ANALYTICAL CHEMISTRY

About the Authors

Dr. P. Saravana Pandian Presently working as Professor (Soil Science and Agricultural Chemistry) at Department of Soil and Environment, Agricultural College and Research Institute, Tamil Nadu Agricultural University Madurai. Before joining University he served as Agricultural Research Scientist in Indian Council of Agricultural Research, New Delhi. He has got 25 years of Teaching, Research and Extension experience in TNAU. His field of specialisation is Soil Chemistry and Fertility. He has been awarded with Best Teacher Award by TNAU during the year 2009. He has published 53 research articles in peer reviewed national and international journals, 2 books, 70 popular articles and presented 40 research papers in National/International seminar and Symposia.

Dr. G. Sridevi Presently working as Assistant Professor (Soil Science and Agricultural Chemistry) at Department of Soil Science and Agricultural Chemistry, Tamil Nadu Agricultural University, Coimbatore, has 6 years of Teaching, Research and Extension experience in TNAU. She has specialization in soil fertility and waste water management. She has published 10 Research articles. 1 book and 13 popular article. Presented 10 research papers in National/International seminar and Symposia.

Dr. R. Indirani Presently working as Assistant Professor (Soil Science and Agricultural Chemistry) at Department of Soil and Environment, Agricultural College and Research Institute, Tamil Nadu Agricultural University Madurai, has 12 years of Teaching, Research and Extension experience in TNAU. She has specialization in soil fertility and plant nutrition, She has published 20 research articles 1 book and 15 popular articles. Presented 20 research papers in National/International seminar and symposia.

Dr. U. Surendran working as Senior Scientist (Soil Science) at Centre for Water Resources Development and Management (CWRDM), Kerala, India. He has got 14 years of Research and Extension experience in R&D Centre, EID Parry (I) Ltd and CWDRM, Kerala. His field of specialisation is Nutrient budgeting and carbon sequestration. He has been awarded with Best Doctoral dissertation in fertilizer usage from Fertilizer Association of India (FAI), New Delhi. He has published 58 research articles in peer reviewed national and international journals, 2 books, 10 book chapters, 10 popular articles and presented 30 research papers in National/International seminar and symposia

Analytical Chemistry An Introduction

P. Saravana Pandian
Professor (Soil Science and Agricultural Chemistry)
Department of Soils and Environment
Agricultural College and Research Institute
Tamil Nadu Agricultural University, Madurai
Tamil Nadu, India

G. Sridevi
Assistant Professor (Soil Science and Agricultural Chemistry)
Department of Soil Science and Agricultural Chemistry
Tamil Nadu Agricultural University, Coimbatore
Tamil Nadu, India

R. Indirani
Assistant Professor (Soil Science and Agricultural Chemistry)
Department of Soils and Environment
Agricultural College and Research Institute
Tamil Nadu Agricultural University, Madurai
Tamil Nadu, India

U. Surendran
Senior Scientist (Soil Science)
Centre for Water Resources Development and Management (CWRDM)
Kerala, India

NEW INDIA PUBLISHING AGENCY
New Delhi – 110 034

NEW INDIA PUBLISHING AGENCY

101, Vikas Surya Plaza, CU Block, LSC Market
Pitam Pura, New Delhi – 110 034, India
Email: info@nipabooks.com
Web: www.nipabooks.com

For customer assistance, please contact
Phone: + 91-11-27 34 17 17 Fax: + 91-11- 27 34 16 16
E-Mail: feedbacks@nipabooks.com

ISBN : 978-81-94766-88-9

Composed and Designed by NIPA.

KERALA AGRICULTURAL UNIVERSITY

Main Campus, Kerala Agriculture University P.O. Thrissur - 680 656, Kerala

Professor K.V. Peter

Ph.D., FNAAS, FNASc FNABS. FISVeg, FISGen., FHSI H.FCHAI FISNS

Former Vice-Chancellor: Kerala Agricultural University and Former Director, ICAR-IISR, Calicut, Kerala

Phone: (R) 0487-2373017 (M) 9446513017

E-mail: *kvptr@yahoo.com; peter.kv@gmail.com*

Foreword

Analytical Chemistry is an applied branch of the science of chemistry that deals with the use of instruments and methods to separate and identify matter(s). In practice separation, identification or quantification may constitute the entire analysis or be combined with another method. Qualitative analysis identifies analyte(s), while the quantitative analysis determines the numerical value or concentration.

Analytical Chemistry consists of classical chemical methods and modern instrumental methods. Classical qualitative methods use separation such as precipitation, extraction and distillation. Identification may be based on difference in colour, odor, melting point, boiling point, radioactivity or reactivity. Classical quantitative analysis uses mass or volume changes to quantify amount. Instrumental methods may be used to separate and or to quantify the samples using instruments such as spectrophotometry, chromatography *etc.*, The qualitative and quantitative analysis can be performed often with the same instrument and may use light energy interaction, heat interaction, electric fields or magnetic fields. Often the same instrument can separate, identify and quantify an analyte.

In scientific fields analysing the constituents is very much essential in order to identify, characterize and quantify the constituents. Analytical chemistry has broad applications to medicine, science and engineering.

The text book "Analytical Chemistry: An Introduction" comprises 19 chapters covering different aspects of analysis. The different aspects are basic principles, analytical tools and apparatus. Volumetric, gravimetric and instrumental methods, radiation methods etc., are explained very well in an easily understandable manner. The interpretation of subject matter ineach chapter of this book has been made carefully and systematically by the authors giving much more emphasis on the requirements at the undergraduate level. This book is a comprehensive one and meets the growing needs of science students. The authors have rich experience in teaching and research and as such presented the subject matter critically and in a lucid language.

I hope this text book would be much value for the students of Chemistry, Biology, Agriculture, Geology, Medicine, Engineering etc., Authors are well known scientists in applied chemistry.

I congratulate the eminent authors for a modern text book. The publisher New India Publishing Agency, New Delhi is well known for its zero error publishing of text books. I congratulate the publisher as well.

(K V Peter)

Preface

Analysis of any constituents qualitatively and quantitatively is important to any scientific field. Analytical chemistry is a collection of analytical methods. It is an approach to study chemical problems. It is the ideal place in the undergraduate curriculum in science for explaining topics such as common laboratory tools and apparatus, volumetric, gravimetric and instrumental methods. Analytical methods may come and go but the practice for designing and validating analytical methods are universal. Our goal in preparing this text book is to find a more appropriate balance between classical and modern analytical methods. Therefore in order to understand the basic analytical principles, various analytical methods such as volumetry, gravimetry and instrumental methods this book has been written in simple and lucid manner to meet out the requirements of students at undergraduate level. We hope that the students find this text book as a valuable valuable resource throughout their career.

Authors

Contents

Chapter 1

General Principles of Analytical Chemistry

Analytical Chemistry

The science involving the determination of the constituents in terms of elements and compounds is called Analytical Chemistry. It is used to identify the substances found in a material and to quantify the exact amount of substances in them.

The basic principles involved in Analytical Chemistry are changes takes place in the substances by the process of combination, decomposition, replacement and double decomposition.

(a) Combination

Here two or more substances are joined to form a more complex compound.

$4FeO + O_2 \rightarrow 2Fe_2O_3$

(b) Decomposition

It is a process of decomposition of complex substance into simpler compounds.

$2H_2O_2 \rightarrow 2H_2O + O_2$

(c) Replacement

It is a process of replacement of one element for another in a compound

$Zn + H_2SO_4 \rightarrow ZnSO_4 + H_2$

$C_6H_5OH + H_2SO_4 \rightarrow C_6H_5HSO_4OH + H_2$

(d) Double decomposition

Here two compounds react with each other and form two new compounds

$C_6H_5COOH + C_2H_5OH \rightarrow C_6H_5COOC_2H_5 + H_2O$

Sub division of Analytical Chemistry

i) Based on nature of constituents to be analysed

(a) Qualitative analysis

Here presence or absence of a particular substance will be known

Eg. Presence of chloride in irrigation water

Presence of sulphate in ferrous sulphate ($FeSO_4$)

(b) Quantitative analysis

It is the process of determining the amount of constituents present in a compound or mixture

Eg. Amount of chloride present in irrigation water

Amount of starch present in maize grain

ii) Based on the quantity of sample required for analysis

a)	Macro analysis	> 0.1g
b)	Semi micro analysis	0.01-0.1g
c)	Micro analysis	0.001-0.01g
d)	Sub micro analysis	< 0.001g

iii) Based on number of constituents to be analysed

a) Complete analysis

When all the constituents are analysed in a compound, it is called as complete analysis.

Eg. i) Estimation of Fe and SO_4 in $FeSO_4$

ii) Estimation of all the cations and anions in irrigation water

b) Partial analysis

If one or more constituents are analysed in a compound, it is called as partial analysis.

Eg. i) Estimation of chloride in water sample

ii) Estimation of sulphur containing amino acids alone in pulse grain

iv) Based on nature of constituents to be analysed

(a) Proximate analysis

Analysis of major fractions in a compound or mixture is called proximate analysis

Eg. Estimation of starch, proteins, amino acids and sugars

(b) Ultimate analysis

Analysis of elements like C,H, O, N,P,K, Ca etc in a sample

Various analytical methods

i) Qualitative analysis

(a) Flame test

Here the paste of salt is prepared and shown in the flame and based on the colour emitted, the presence or absence of constituents are analysed

Eg. i) Appearance of brick red colour– presence of calcium

ii) Appearance of yellow colour – presence of sodium

iii) Appearance of blue/lilac colour– presence of potassium

iv) Appearance of apple green colour– presence of barium

v) Appearance of blue colour– presence of copper

ii) Quantitative analysis

Various analytical methods are followed for quantifying proximate and or ultimate constituents present in an element, compound or mixture

a) Neutralisation

An acid react with a base gives rise to salt and water. If a standard base is utilized for the determination of an unknown acid, it is referred as acidimetry and the determination of an unknown base using a standard acid is called a alkalimetry.

b) Precipitation method

It is a volumetric method which results in the formation of precipitate

Eg. Determination of chloride in irrigation water sample

$NaCl + AgNO_3 \rightarrow AgCl + NaNO_3$

$2AgCl + K_2CrO_4 \rightarrow Ag_2CrO_4 + 2KCl$

(Brick red colour precipitate)

c) Complex formation

This involves complex formation or chelating agents which make coordinate bond with metallic cation.

Eg. Estimation of Ca and Mg by EDTA

d) Gravimetry

Here the quantity of reaction product is measured by taking the weight.

Eg. Estimation of sulphate in water sample

e) Conductometry

It deals with the measurement of electrical conductivity and resistance of a substance. It is based on Ohm's law.

f) Voltametry

It involves the measurement of potential of microelectrode at a particular voltage.

g) Potentiometry

It is the measurement of potential developed in an electrode based on the activity of ions.

h) Colorimetry/Spectrophotometry

It is based on the comparison of colour developed by the addition of specific reagents.

i) Flame photometry

Here the sample is injected as a fine mist on a flame and based on the intensities of light emitted, the amount of substance is measured. Intensity of light emitted is directly proportional to the amount of substance present.

Some concepts

i) Precision and Accuracy

Precision

It is the degree of agreement between measured values and other values obtained under same condition. It refers to the reproducibility of results.

Accuracy

It is the degree of agreement between the measured value and the true value. It refers to the reliability of the results.

ii) Errors

Errors refer to the numerical difference between the measured value and true value. There are five types of errors

a) Absolute error (E)

This is the difference between observed or measured value (O) and the true value (T) of the quantity measured.

Absolute error = True value(T) – Observed value (O)

Eg. Estimated water soluble P_2O_5 content of Single super phosphate is 15 % but the true value is 16%

b) Relative error

It is the ratio of absolute error and the true value. It is referred as percentage.

$$\text{Relative error} = \frac{\text{Absolute error}}{\text{True value}} \times 100$$

Eg . Estimated water soluble P_2O_5 content of Single super phosphate is 15% while the true value is 16%

$$\text{Relative error} = \frac{1}{16} \times 100 = 6.25\%$$

c) Determinate error

Errors that can be determined and eliminated or reduced to the minimum by following certain techniques. Determinate errors are grouped into 6 categories.

i) Physical error

Error occur by physical means while analysing, any substances like loss of materials during washing,filtration/transfer etc.,

ii) Personal error

It is due to the person who is analyzing the constituents.

Eg. Incorrect method of sampling, taking weight of sample, lack of knowledge on analysis

iii) Errors in methods

Errors which occur due to the incorrect method of sampling, wrong choice of a reaction etc.

iv) Instrumental errors

This error is due to the fault on the instrument, electric power fluctuation etc.,

v) Proportional errors

It depends on the purity of a standard compound. If any impurities present in the substances that will affect the true value of the constituents to be analysed in a substance.

vi) Crude errors

These errors are due to the use of numerically incorrect conversion factors.

Application of Analytical Chemistry

a) Agriculture

Analytical Chemistry provides estimation of soil, water, manures, fertilizers and proximate and ultimate constituents of plant samples

b) Medical field

It is used in clinical laboratory tests to diagnose the diseases

c) Industries

Analytical chemistry is used to test the quality of materials as well as the finished products

d) Pharmaceutical industries

Analytical chemistry is used in the quality and quantity of inputs used in the preparation of drugs and to test the quality and quantity of ingredients in the finished drugs.

Chapter 2

Study of Common Laboratory Glasswares and Apparatus

Laboratory analysis is an important part in any branch of chemistry and analytical chemistry in particular. To undertake the analysis, both apparatus and equipments are needed.

Analytical tools

- Analytical apparatus
- Equipments

Different types of tools (or) apparatus are commonly employed in various volumetric and gravimetric analysis.

Analytical apparatus

- Major volumetric apparatus
- Accessory volumetric apparatus
- Gravimetric apparatus
- Miscellaneous

I. Major Volumetric Apparatus

1. Pipette

Pipettes are used to deliver a definite volume of solution precisely. There are 4 kinds of pipettes.

i) Volumetric pipette

- It is used to deliver a definite volume of liquid under specified conditions.
- It consist of a mark that shows the volume of the pipette.

- Some of the pipettes have safety bulb which is commonly used to pipette out weak acids (or) bases.
- Volumetric pipettes available in different capacities ranging from 1 to 100ml (1, 5, 10, 20, 25, 50 and 100ml)

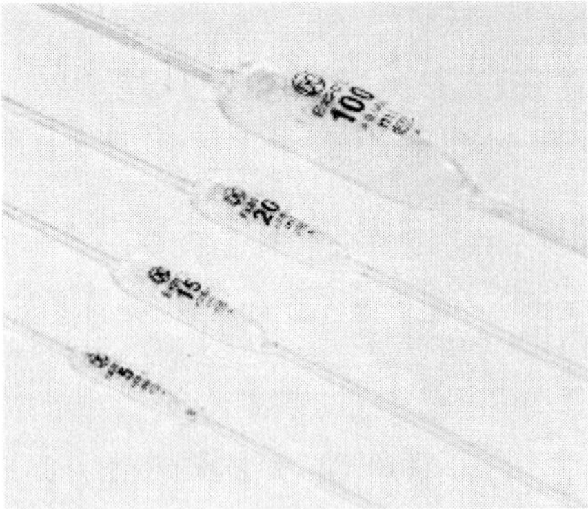

(i) Graduated pipette

- Stems are graduated
- These are used to deliver various small volumes of liquid based on our discretion
- They are available at different capacities ranging from 1 to 20 ml (1, 2, 5, 10, 20 ml)
- They are less precise than volumetric pipettes

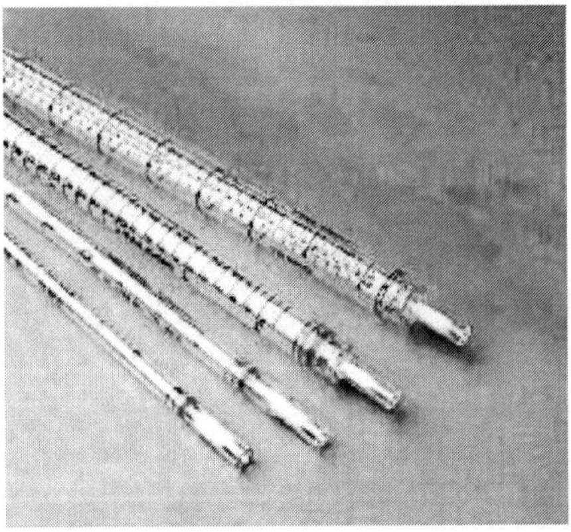

(ii) Robinson pipette

- It is available with a capacity of 20ml
- It is used to deliver the soil water suspension while estimating soil texture by mechanical analysis.

- It has two way opening viz., inlet and outlet.
- The outlet is used to remove the excess solution pipetted out.

(iii) Micro pipette

- They are constructed with capacities ranging from 10 to 100 lambda
- It is mainly used to transfer the solution in biochemical analysis / biotechnology analysis.

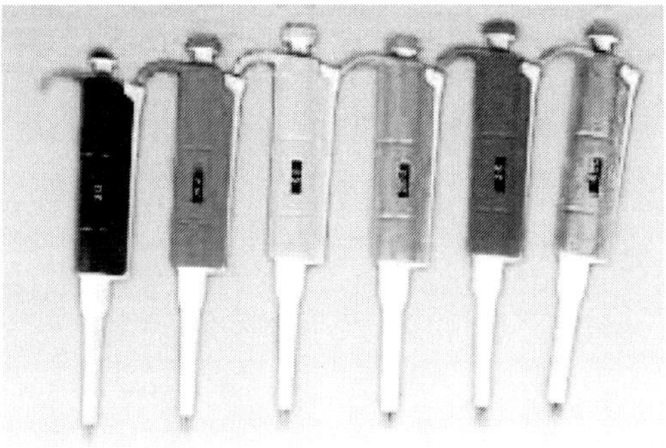

2.Burette

- It is used while undertaking titrimetric analysis.
- It is available in different capacities ranging from 10 to 100 ml.
- 50 ml burette is commonly used in the Laboratory.
- It has a stop-cock to stop the delivery of solution during titrimetric analysis.

3.Measuring cylinder

- They are graduated vessels with a broad base
- They are used to measure the liquid approximately
- They are available in different capacities ranging from 5 ml to 1 litre (5, 10, 20, 25, 50, 100, 250, 500 and 1000 ml).

4. Volumetric flask

- It is a flat – bottomed shaped vessel with a long narrow neck
- A mark in the neck indicates the volume that it holds.
- They are used to prepare the standard solutions viz., Molar, Normal, Percentage, ppm solutions etc.

- They are available in different capacities ranging from 5 ml to 2000 ml

II Accessory Volumetric Appartus

There are certain laboratory glass wares which are used to transfer solutions from one vessel to another to perform titrations and other operations.

(i) Conical flask

- They are useful in performing titrations
- The narrow neck of the flask prevents the entry of external agents like O_2 and CO_2 etc.
- Conical flasks are available in different capacities viz., 50, 100, 250 and 500 ml.
- Conical flasks are also used for digestion of plant, manure and fertilizer samples.

(ii) Beaker

- They are available in various sizes ranging from 25 to 1000 ml (25, 50, 100, 250, 400, 500 and 1000 ml).
- They are provided with a spout to transfer the solutions

There are two types of beakers

(a) Low form beaker

- Low form beakers are used to transfer the solutions

(b) Tall form beaker

- Tall form beakers are used in distillation.

(iii) Funnel

- They are useful for filtration and transfer of liquid to narrow necked vessels.
- The funnels are available with various diameters of 5, 7.5 and 9 cm.

(iv) Porcelain basin and porcelain crucibles

- They are used for evaporating and concentrating solutions at low temperature

(v) All glass wash bottles

- They are useful to keep and deliver hot and cold distilled water

(vi) Squeeze bottle

- They are used to keep and deliver distilled water and diluted acids like 10% HCl, 0.1 N HCl etc.

III. Gravimetric apparatus

- The materials used in gravimetric analysis are known as gravimetric apparatus.

(i) Buchner funnel

- It is made up of porecelain and is fitted with a porous disc
- One or two good quality filter papers are placed on the porous disc and the filtration is done by suction.

(ii) Filter flask/Erlenmeyor flask

- They are conical flask fitted with a side vent which can be attached to a vacuum pump to create vacuum in the conical flask during filtration.

(iii) Silica basin and silica crucible

- They are used to make ash of any substance at high temperature
- They can with stand upto 1200°C
- They are also used for ignition of precipitates.

IV. Miscellaneous apparatus

(1) Bunsen burner

- It was discovered by Robert Bunsen
- It is used for heating, sterilization and combustion etc

(2) Clay pipe triangle

- It is used to support items being heated by a bunsen burner
- It is made up of clay (or) ceramic tubes

(3) Liebig condenser

- It is used to condense the gas into liquid during distillation
- It has outlet and inlet wherein continuous flow of water will be there

(4) Distillation flask

- It is a round bottomed flask used in distillation

5. Dropping bottle

- It is used to supply liquids in drops
- It is mainly used to store indicators

6. Glass rod

- It is used to stir the substances while dissolving
- It is also used to transfer solutions from one container to another

7. Policeman glass rod

- A small hand-held flexible natural rubber scraper attached to a glass rod used in chemical laboratories to transfer residues (or) precipitates.

8. Iodine flask

- It is used in Iodine estimation

9. Kjeldahl flask

- It has a pear shaped bottom with a long neck
- It is used for digestion of soil, manure and fertilizer samples.

10. Moisture bottle

- It is made up of glass with a tightly fitting lid
- It is used in estimation of moisture content of soil, plant, manure and fertilizer samples.

11. Pestle and Mortar

- They are made up of clay
- They are used to grind the samples (or) indicator substances

12. Porcelain tile

- They are resistant to chemicals
- They are used to identify the colour change clearly during titration

13. Reagent bottle

- It ranges from 100 ml to even 25 litres
- It is used to store the reagents during laboratory analysis

14. Rubber cork

- It is used to plug glass containers especially distillation flask to provide an air tight condition.

15. Separating funnel

- It is used to separate two immiscible liquids based on difference in density.

16. Shaking bottle

- It is made up of plastic and is used to extract elements / compounds by shaking with suitable extractants.

17. Sieve

- It is used to get the particles of desired size (2mm and 0.5 mm sieve)
- Normally it is used to sieve the soil samples

18. Spatula

- It is used to mix, spread and take chemicals

19. Test tube

- It is available both in glass and plastic
- It is used to hold, mix (or) heat small quantities of liquids

20. Test tube holder

- It is made up of metal with wooden handle
- It is used to hold the test tube while heating the test tubes

21. Tongs

- They are used for gripping and lifting containers when they are hot.

22. Watch glass

- It is used to evaporate liquids
- To hold solids
- It is also used to cover the beakers

23. Wind screen

- It is made up of iron
- It is used to curtail the turbulence in the flame caused by wind during distillation

24. Wire gauze

- It is used to support a container on a bunsen burner
- It prevents the direct contact between the glass container and the flame during heating.

25. Burette stand

- It is used to hold burette during and after titrations

26. Filter stand

- It is made up of wood (or) plastic (or) iron
- The height is adjustable and is used to hold funnel during filtrations.

27. Tripod stand

- It is a three legged structure made up of steel
- It is used to hold beakers /conical flasks / silica basins/silica crucibles during heating by bunsen burner.

28. Potash basin

- It is used to mix the samples and reagents

Equipments

1. Hot air – oven

- It is used to dry soil and plant samples
- The temperature range normally between 30 and 250 °C
- It has a heating mantle to produce heat
- The plant samples are dried at 60 to 70 °C and the soil samples at 105 °C usually for 8-10 hours.
- Hot air oven should not be opened while switch on.

2. Muffle furnace

- This can produce a heat ranging from 200 to 1200 °C
- It is used for ashing the biological and chemical samples
- The samples for ignition is taken in silica basin (or) crucibles.

3. Water bath

- It is an electrically operated instrument meant for boiling the samples taken in basins / beakers /conical flaks by the steam generated due to boiling of water.

4. Hot plate

- It is a plat form like instrument used to heat and digest the samples slowly and steadily.
- This has heating coils
- Inbetween the plat form and the sample a thin layer of sand is spread for uniform conduction of heat.

5. Desiccator

- Hot crucibles / moisture bottles are usually cooled inside the desiccator before weighing
- It is filled with some drying agents (or) desiccants like anhydrous $CaCl_2$, silica gel.

6. Water still

- It is used for distilling the water used for various experiments

7. Mechanical shaker

- This is useful for shaking the samples with solutions / extractants for a specified time
- It has an electrical motor fitted to a shaking device

8. Mechanical stirrer

- This is an electrical instrument used to stirr the contents of vessel particularly useful for soil textural analysis.

9. Centrifuge

- It is used to separate the precipitates and insoluble materials by centrifugal force

- Manually driven and electrically operated centrifuges are commonly used in the laboratories

10. Wiley Mill (Grinder)

- It is an electrical instrument used for grinding / powdering the samples
- Normally it is used for powdering the plant samples.

Chapter 3

Basic Concepts of Preparation of Standard Solutions

Standard solutions

Standard solutions are solutions of accurately known concentration

Different standard solutions are

a) Molar solution

b) Molal solution

c) Formula weight solutions

d) Normal solution

e) Percentage solution

f) ppm solution

(a) Molar solution

1 gram molecular weight of substance dissolved in water and the volume made upto 1000 ml

Molecular weight

It is defined as the sum of atomic weight of elements present in a compound

Example:

Preparation of 1000 ml of 1 Molar NaOH. Molecular weight of NaOH = 40 g (23+16+1).

Therefore 40 gram of NaOH is dissolved in water and made upto 1000 ml will give 1 M NaOH solution

(b) Molal solution

1 gram molecular weight of substance dissolved in water and made upto 1 kg. It is weight/weight (w/w)

(c) Formula weight solution

1 gram formula weight of substance dissolved in water and made upto 1000 ml is called formula weight solution

Example

$FeSO_4$

Molecular weight of $FeSO_4$ = 152 g

Fe = 56

S = 32

4 O = 64

152

But $FeSO_4$ is supplied as hydrated form also

It is available as $FeSO_4 . 7H_2O$

Molecular weight of $FeSO_4 . 7H_2O$ = 278 g

Therefore, 278 g of $FeSO_4 . 7H_2O$ dissolved in water and volume made upto 1000ml will give 1 M $FeSO_4 . 7H_2O$ solution.

(d) Normal solution

1 gram equivalent weight of a substance dissolved in water and volume made upto 1000 ml will give one normal solution.

Equivalent weight

(1) Equivalent weight of an element

$$= \frac{\text{Atomic weight}}{\text{Valency}}$$

Example

Equivalent weight of oxygen

Atomic weight of O is 16

Valency of O is 2

$$\text{Equivalent weight} = \frac{16}{2} = 8 \text{ gram}$$

(ii) Equivalent weight of an acid

$$\text{Equivalent weight} = \frac{\text{Molecular weight}}{\text{Basicity}}$$

Basicity is number of replaceable H in an acid

Example

Equivalent weight of H_2SO_4

Molecular weight of H_2SO_4 = 98 g

2H = 2

S = 32

4O = 64

98g

Number of replaceable H in H_2SO_4 = 2

$$\text{Equivalent weight of } H_2SO_4 = \frac{98}{2} = 49 \text{ g}$$

(iii) Equivalent weight of a base

$$\text{Equivalent weight of base} = \frac{\text{Molecular weight}}{\text{Acidity}}$$

Acidity is number of replaceable OH in a base

Example

Equivalent weight of KOH

Molecular weight of KOH = 56 g

K = 39

O = 16

H = 1

56 g

Number of replaceable OH in KOH =1

Equivalent weight of KOH = $\frac{56}{1}$ = 56 g

(iv) Equivalent weight of salt

Equivalent weight of a salt is that it combines with one equivalent of acid (or) base

Example

$Na_2CO_3 + 2HCl \longrightarrow 2\ NaCl + CO_2 + H_2O$

1 mole of Na_2CO_3 reacts with 2 mole of HCl

Molecular weight of Na_2CO_3 = 106 g

2 Na = 2x23 = 46

C = 1x12 = 12

3 O = 3x16 = 48

106g

106 parts by weight of Na_2CO_3 reacts with 2x36.46 parts by weight of HCl (2 mole HCl). Therefore, one equivalent of HCl reacts with

$$\frac{106}{2 \times 36.46} \times 36.46 = 53g$$

(v) Equivalent weight of an oxidising agent

Equivalent weight of an oxidising agent is that it gives 8 parts by weight of oxygen for oxidation purpose.

Example

Acidified $KMnO_4$ is a strong oxidising agent.

$$2KMnO_4 + 3H_2SO_4 \longrightarrow K_2SO_4 + 2MnSO_4 + 3H_2O + 5(O)$$

Molecular weight of $KMnO_4$ is = 158g

K = 39

Mn = 55

4O = 64

158g

Here 2 mole of $KMnO_4$ is reacting therefore 2 x 158 g = 316 g

5 nascent oxygen is released during the above said oxidation reaction so 5x16 = 80g

80 parts of weight of oxygen is contributed by 316 parts by weight of $KMnO_4$

Therefore, 8 parts by weight of oxygen is contributed by = $\frac{316 \times 8}{80}$ = 31.6g

Equivalent weight of $KMnO_4$ =31.6 g

(vii) Equivalent weight of a reducing agent

Equivalent weight of a reducing agent is that it takes 8 parts by weight of oxygen for reduction purpose

Example

$FeSO_4$ is a reducing agent

$$2FeSO_4 + H_2SO_4 + (O) \longrightarrow 2Fe_2(SO_4)_3 + H_2O$$

Molecular weight of $FeSO_4$ = 152g

Fe = 56

S = 32

4O = 64

152 g

16 parts of weight of oxygen is taken up by 2x152 g (2 Mole $FeSO_4$ is reacting) parts by weight of $FeSO_4$ / therefore 8 parts by weight of oxygen is taken up by

$$= \frac{2x152 \times 8}{16} = 152 \text{ g}$$

Equivalent weight of $FeSO_4$ =152 g

ppm

One **ppm** is equivalent to 1 milligram of any substance per liter of water (mg/l) or 1 milligram of substance per kilogram (mg/kg)

Per cent solution

1 gram of substance dissolved in water/any solvent and the volume made upto 100ml

Primary standard solutions

Principle

A known quantity of the substance is dissolved in water and made upto the mark in the volumetric flask. Standard solutions prepared in this way are known as primary standards.

Preparation of primary standard solutions

Example

Preparation of 1000 ml of 0.1 Na_2CO_3

Molecular weight of Na_2CO_3 = 106 g

$$Na_2CO_3 + 2HCl \longrightarrow 2NaCl + CO_2 + H_2O$$

106 parts of weight of Na_2CO_3 reacts with

2x36.46 parts of weight of HCl

$$\text{1 equivalent of HCl reacts with} = \frac{106}{2 \times 33.46} \times 35.46$$

Equivalent weight of Na_2CO_3 =53 g

53 gram of Na_2CO_3 is dissolved in water and made upto 1000 ml gives 1 N Na_2CO_3

5.3g Na_2CO_3 dissolved in water and made upto 1000 ml gives 0.1 N Na_2CO_3

Materials Required

AR grade Na_2CO_3

1000 ml volumetric flask

400 ml beaker

Funnel

Electronic balance

Glass rod

Procedure

- Weigh exactly 5.3 g of AR grade Na_2CO_3 (oven dried at 110°C)
- Transfer it into a 400 ml beaker add about 200 ml of distilled water, stirr it well with a glass rod.
- Transfer the solution into a 1000 ml volumetric flask through a funnel slowly.
- Add distilled water into the beaker are stirr it well and transfer the solution into the 1000 ml volumetric flask.
- Make up the volume to 1000 ml mark with distilled water.
- Mix the solutions thoroughly to get the homogeneity.
- Label the solution and preserve it for future work. The label should contain name of the chemical, normality, date of preparation and person who prepared the solution.

Chapter 4

Volumetric Analysis: Principles Preparation of Primary Standard Solutions

Volumetric Analysis

- Measurement of volume of reagents required for the completion of reactions
- Also called titrimetry – most widely used techniques of chemical analysis
- Rapid, accurate, convenient and inexpensive

Principle of Volumetric analysis

- Law of chemical equivalent/law of volumetric analysis
- At equivalent point of titration, the number of equivalents of standard is exactly equal to the number of equivalents of a substance with which it has reacted
- $V_1N_1 = V_2N_2$ – Product of volume and normality of reactant 1 is equal to the volume and normality of reactant 2

Example

10 ml of 0.1N Na_2CO_3 = 10 ml of 0.1N H_2SO_4

Pre requisites for volumetric analysis

- The reaction should be stoichiometric
- The reaction should be specific without any side reactions
- No interference – if any they should be marked/ removed before titration
- Reaction should be fast

- There should not be any reverse reactions
- Marked change in some properties of the solution at the end of the reaction

Titration

- Process of determining the volume of a substance required to just complete the reaction with known volume of other substance

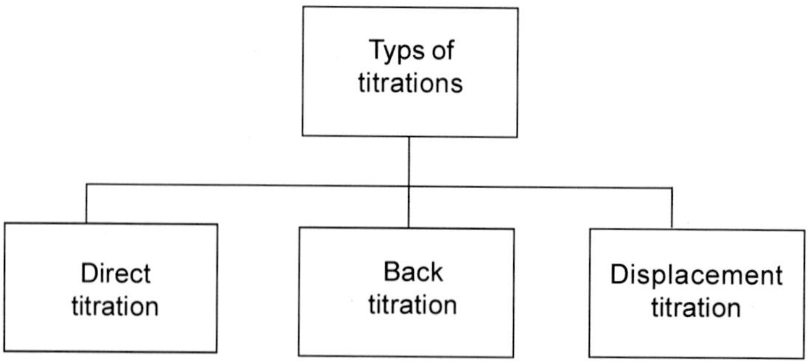

- From the volume of the standard solution, the volume of the test solution is calculated

Methods of titration

i. Direct titration

The solution under test is directly titrated with a standard solution

Example

Na_2CO_3 vs. HCl

KOH vs. $(CH_2COOH)_2$

ii. Back titration

Adding known excess amount of the reagent to the test solution and finding out the excess unreacted part by titration with the third reagent of known concentration

Example

- In N estimation, the NH_3 liberated is collected in a known excess of H_2SO_4 (A)
- A part of H_2SO_4 is used to absorb evolved NH_3

- The remaining H_2SO_4 (B) is determined by back titration with KOH
- The difference of A-B gives the actual amount of H_2SO_4 used to absorb the NH_3

iii. Displacement titration

- The ion to be determined is first converted to some other chemical compound
- Then titrated directly with a standard solution

Example

Iodometry

Requirements of a titration

- Reactions must be stoichiometric
- Reactions must be rapid
- Reactions should be specific and no side reactions
- When the reaction is complete, there should be marked change in some properties of the solution like colour change brought about by indicator/ pH range
- End point should be reproducible
- No reverse reaction
- Equilibrium should shift far towards the right side of the reaction

Primary standard solution

- A standard solution is prepared by dissolving an accurately weighed quantity of a highly pure chemical is called primary standard
- Primary standard solutions – Definite and known strength

Requirement of a chemical to be primary standard

- Substances must be chemically pure with high degree of purity

  $$2\,HCl + Na_2CO_3 \longrightarrow 2NaCl + CO_2 + H_2O$$

- Impurities should not be more than 0.05%
- Must be staple on keeping both in solid and solution states.
- Non hygroscopic and not easily affected by acid fumes and CO_2

- Gram equivalent of the chemical should be as large as possible, so that the precision in determining the normality of the solution is high
- Substance must withstand fairly high temperature
- Primary standard is dried before weighing
- Moisture is removed at 100-110 °C
- Dissolution constant for acids should be high so that distribution will be rapid and uniform
- Must be freely soluble
- Solid and crystalline

Examples of Primary standard

I. Acid base titration

Acids : Succinic acid, Potassium hydrogen pthalate

Bases : Na_2CO_3, Borax

II. Redox titration

Oxidising agents : $K_2Cr_2O_7$, $(COONa)_2$

Reducing Agents : $(COOH)_2$, $Na_2S_2O_3$

III. Salts

NaCl , KCl

Chemicals not prepared as primary standards

- NaOH
- KOH
- $FeSO_4$
- $AgNO_3$
- $MgCl_2$
- $CaCl_2$
- P_2O_5
- H_2SO_4
- HCl

Chapter 5

Volumetric Analysis- Preparation of Secondary Standard Solutions and Standardisation

Secondary standard solution

- Solution of chemicals which lack one (or) all the properties for a primary standard
- A solution standardised by titrating a primary standard
- Less accurate than a primary standard
- 1N, 0.5N, 0.1 N etc

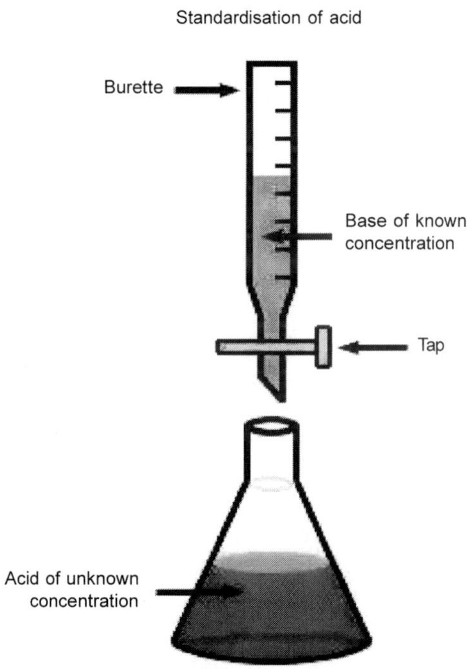

Preparation

- Quantity of the chemical required is calculated from the equivalent weight
- A slightly higher amount of the chemical is weighed to provide allowances for decomposition, impurities, dilution etc.
- Transferred to a 250 ml beaker, small amount of water is added and stirred with a glass rod
- Transfer into a volumetric flask and made up to known volume
- Standardise against a primary standard using appropriate indicators and exact normality is calculated

Standardisation

- Process of determining accurate strength
- Approximately prepared secondary standard solution by titrating against a primary standard using suitable indicator
- Dilution/concentration techniques

Volumetric standardisation

Secondary standard	Primary standard	Indicator
I. Acids		
HCl and H_2SO_4	Na_2CO_3	Methyl orange/ Methyl red
HNO_3	Borax	Methyl orange/ Methyl red
II. Bases		
NaOH and KOH	Potassium hydrogen phthalate, succinic acid	Phenolphthalein
$Ca(OH)_2$	Benzoic acid	Phenolphthalein
III. Oxidising agents		
$KMnO_4$	Oxalic acid Sodium oxalate	Self indicator
IV. Reducing agents		
Ferrous sulphate, Ferrous Ammonium sulphate	$K_2Cr_2O_7$	Diphenyl amine (internal indicator)
Iodine	Arsenic oxide (As_2O_3)	Starch
Sodium thiosulphate	KIO_3	Starch
V. Others		
$AgNO_3$	NaCl	Potasium chromate (K_2CrO_4)
KSCN	$AgNO_3$	Ferric alum
EDTA	$CaCO_3$ in HCl	Murexide
Sodium thiosulphate	Copper	Starch

Advantages of volumetric analysis

- Handy and tedious operations are not involved
- More rapid and time saving
- Fairly accurate
- Economical involves less cost of chemicals and apparatus
- Minute quantities which can be determined easily
- Possible to estimate one (or) more constituents of a substance without separations
- Standardization of acid and base should be included

Chapter 6

Theory of Indicators and Buffers

Indicator

- A substance which indicates the end point on completion of the reaction.
- Helps in the visual determination of the completion of titration.

Types of indicators

i) Internal indicators

a. Indicators used in acid-base (Neutralization) reaction

b. Indicators used in precipitation reaction

c. Indicator used in oxidation- reduction reaction (Redox indicator)

d. Indicators used in complexometry (Metal indicators / Metallochromic indicators)

ii) External indicators

iii) Self indicator

iv) Adsorption and complex forming indicators

v) Mixed indicator

vi) Universal indicator

vii) pH test papers

i) Internal indicator

- Indicator added in the solution where reaction occurs is called internal indicator.
- Gives clear visual change in the solution being titrated.

Example

Methyl red, Methyl orange, Phenolphthalein, Methylene blue, Diphenylamine

Four groups of internal indicator

a) Indicators used in acid-base (Neutralization) reaction

- The H^+ indicators (acid-base) are organic dyes (Weak organic acids/ base)
- Changes colour with variation in pH value.
- Colour change from an acid to alkaline is not sudden and abrupt, takes place within a small interval of pH - change.

Example

Methyl orange, Phenolphthalein, Methyl red, Bromothymol blue

Suitability of indicator

Types of titration	Example	Suitable indicator	pH range of colour change
Strong acid vs Strong base	NaOH vs HCl NaOH vs H_2SO_4 KOH vs HCl	Methyl orange Methyl red Phenolphthalein	5 to 10
Strong acid vs Weak base	HCl vs Na_2CO_3 HCl vs $NaHCO_3$ HCl vs $Ca(OH)_2$ H_2SO_4 vs Na_2CO_3	Methyl orange Methyl red	4 to 6
Weak acid vs Strong base	CH_3COOH vs NaOH $(CH_2COOH)_2$ vs KOH	Methyl orange Methyl red	8 to 10
Weak acid vs Weak base	CH_3COOH vs Na_2CO_3 CH_3COOH vs $NaHCO_3$	No suitable indicator	Slowly change of H

b) Indicators used in precipitation reaction

- The end point of completion of titration is formation of precipitates
- Used in determination of Cl, Br and I

Example

- Titration of NaCl with $AgNO_3$ with K_2CrO_4 as indicator
- End point: Formation of brick red colour precipitate (Ag_2CrO_4)

$$NaCl + AgNO_3 \longrightarrow AgCl + NaNO_3$$

$$2AgCl + K_2CrO_4 \longrightarrow Ag_2CrO_4 + 2KCl$$

c) Indicator used in oxidation- reduction reaction (Redox indicator)

- Redox indicator posses different colour in the oxidized form and different colour in its reduced form

Example Diphenyl amine, Methylene blue, Orthophenanthroline

d) Indicators used in complexometry (Metal indicators / Metallochromic indicators)

- Organic dyes that from stable complexes with metal ions.
- Used to indicate endpoint in a complexation reaction.

Indicators	pH range	Elements estimated
Eriochrome Black T	7.5-10.5	Ba, Ca, Mg, Zn
Murexide	6.0-13.0	Ca, Ni, Cu
Salicylic acid	2.0-3.0	Fe

ii) External indicators

- Indicators not added to the reaction medium
- Kept away from the solution where reaction takes place are called External indicators.

Example

Potassium ferricyanade $K_3(Fe(CN)_6)$ as indicator in the titration of $K_2Cr_2O_7$ and $FeSO_4$ in acid medium.

iii) Self indicator

- In a titration involving two solutions, one of the substance itself act as the indicator.
- Example

$KMnO_4$ Vs Oxalic acid → $KMnO_4$ as indicator

$KMnO_4$ Vs $FeSO_4$ → $KMnO_4$ as indicator

iv) Adsorption and complex forming indicators

- Indicators results in the formation of complex at the end point.

Example

- Titration involving iodine (iodimetry) the starch solution is a indicator.
- It forms a complex with I_2 – gives a dark blue colour.

v) Mixed indicator

- Mixing two or more indicators (or)
- Mixing one indicator with an organic dye to detect the end point more accurately with a narrow range of pH.
- Titrations involving weak acids (or) weak bases , the end point cannot be easily detected using single indicators where mixed indicators are used.

Example

Methyl green and Phenolphthalein (pH 8.4-8.8)

Red violet : pH < 8.4

Grey/pale blue: pH 8.4-8.8

Pink : pH > 8.8

Methyl red + Bromocresol green used in the estimation of available N in soil by Alkaline $KMnO_4$ method.

vi) Universal indicator

- Mixture of two or more indicators.
- Not used in quantitative analysis.
- Used to determine the approximate pH range of a solution.

Available in two ranges

- Narrow : pH range of 0.2 to 0.4 units.
- Wide : pH range of 2 units (6-8, 8-10) .

vii) pH test papers

- Filter papers impregnated with indicators.
- Similar to mixed indicators.

- Used to determine the pH of any solution approximately

Theory of indicators

1) Ostwalds theory

- Proposed by Ostwald in 1891
- Based on Arrhenius theory
- The acid — base indicator is either weak acid or weak base
- They are partially ionized in solution
- Ionized form — different colour
- Unionized form — different colour
- Medium changes ⟶ colour changes

Example

- Phenolphthalein is a weak acid — partially ionized in solution

  $Hph \rightleftharpoons H^+ + ph^-$
- Unionized form — colorless
- Ionized form — pink colour
- While adding phenolphthalein indicator into an acid medium

  $H_2SO_4 \longrightarrow 2H^+ + SO_4^{2-}$

  $Hph \rightleftharpoons H^+ + ph^-$
- H_2SO_4 ionizes into $2H^+$ and SO_4^{2-}
- Due to excess H^+ in acid medium, there would be reverse reaction takes place and unionized form of Hph would be formed due to common ion effect.
- While adding phenolphthalein into a basic medium

  $NaOH \longrightarrow Na^+ + OH^-$
- NaOH ionizes into Na^+ and OH^-
- H^+ of phenolphthalein combine with OH^- and form H_2O and Na^+ and ph^- combine and to form Naph which impart pink colour
- Hence in basic medium phenolphthalein is in ionized form — pink colour

- Phenolphthalein is not a suitable indicator in the titration of strong acid vs weak base
- OH^- produced by the weak base at the endpoint is too low to cause ionization of phenolphthalein
- Hence pink colour does not appear exactly at the equivalence point

Methyl orange

- Methyl orange is a weak base

  $MeOH \longrightarrow Me^+ + OH^-$

- Un ionized form — yellow
- Ionized form — pink
- While adding methyl orange to an alkaline medium

  $NaOH \longrightarrow Na^+ + OH^-$

  $MeOH \longrightarrow Me^+ + OH^-$

- NaOH ionizes into Na^+ and OH^-, OH^- concentration get increased in the product side
- Reverse reaction takes place due to more concentration of OH^- and unionized form of MeOH formed by common ion effect —— yellow colour

In acid medium

$HCl \longrightarrow H^+ + Cl^-$

$MeOH \longrightarrow Me^+ + OH^-$

H^+ combines with OH $\longrightarrow H_2O$

- Acidic solution, indicator is in ionized form — pink colour
- Methyl orange is not a suitable indicator in the titration of strong base vs weak acid
- Weak acid does not furnish sufficient H^+ to shift the equilibrium towards the right

2) Quinonoid / Choromophore theory

- Colour change of an acid-base indicator arises due to structural change

- Colour change — Molecular rearrangement and presence of chromophore
- Radicals / group of double bonds
- NO_2,N_2,CO, quinonoid group

Indicator exist as an equilibrium mixture of two tautomeric forms

forms → Benzoid, Quinonoid

- One form-acidic solution
- Other form-basic solution

Example

a) Phenolphthalein — Tautomeric mixture of 2 forms

Quinonoid form — Alkaline medium — pink colour

Benzoid form — Acid medium — colourless

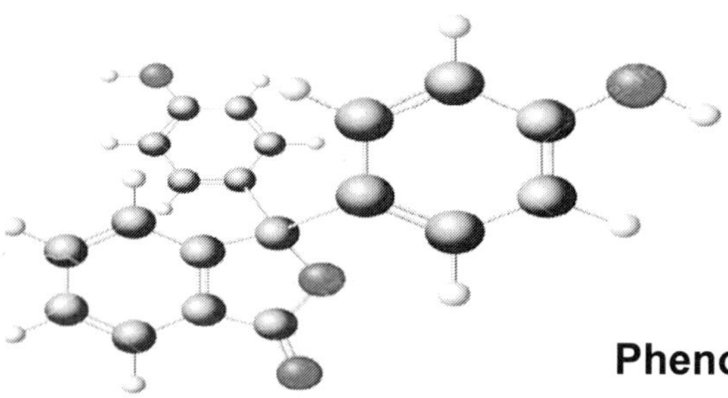

Phenolphthalein

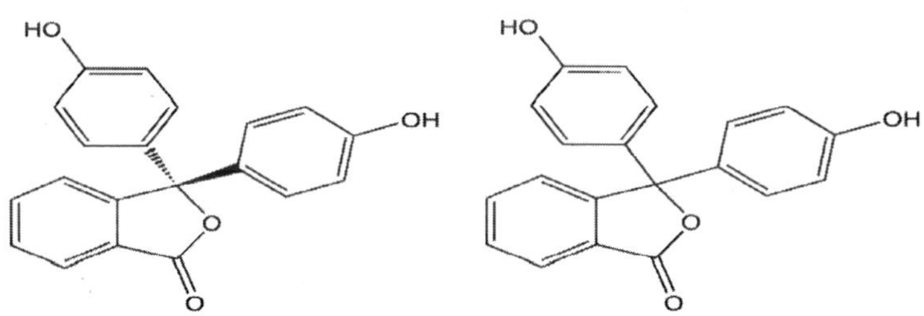

b) Methyl orange

Benzoid form — Alkaline medium — yellow

Quinonoid form — Acidic medium — pink

e.g., HPH:

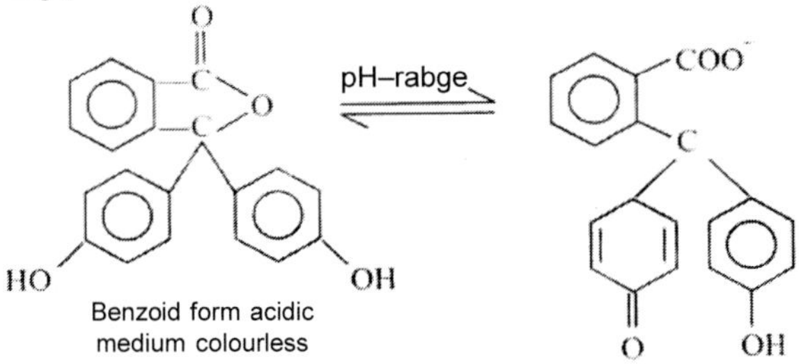

Benzoid form acidic medium colourless

Quinoid form (Pink colour)

Detection of end point

1) Visual methods

a) Titrant itself acts as a self indicator on completion of reaction

$KMnO_4$ — is taken in burette and titrated against $FeSO_4(Fe^{2+})$

When all the Fe^{2+} ions converted to Fe^{3+}, next added drop of $KMnO_4$ — pink colour

$$2\ KMnO_4 + 2H_2SO_4 \longrightarrow K_2SO_4 + MnSO_4 + H_2O + 5(O)$$

$$2FeSO_4 + (O) + H_2SO_4 \longrightarrow Fe_2(SO_4)_3 + H_2O$$

b) A change in colour of the added indicator solution

Titration of HCl and NaOH

Phenolphthalein —— pink colour — alkaline medium

Neutralization is completed, further addition of one drop of HCl – colourless

$$NaOH + HCl \longrightarrow NaCl + H_2O$$

c) Formation of a soluble product

Titration of $HgCl_2$ + KI

Red precipitate of HgI_2 formed which reacts with KI – soluble colourless complex

Disappearance of red precipitate – End point

d) Appearance of a precipitate

Titration of NaCl with $AgNO_3$

Indicator – K_2CrO_4

AgCl formed

A drop of addition of $AgNO_3 - Ag_2CrO_4$

$$NaCl + AgNO_3 \longrightarrow AgCl + NaNO_3$$

$$2AgCl + K_2CrO_4 \longrightarrow \underset{\text{(red precipitate)}}{Ag_2CrO_4} + 2KCl$$

2) Electrical methods

- The end point of titration — change in electrical properties of the titration mixture
- A graph is plotted between the magnitude of electrical properties and corresponding volume of titrant added
- A sudden change in the graph — end point
- Called electrometric titrations

Examples

- Potentiometry (Measurement of potential)
- Conductometry (Measurement of conductance)
- Amperometry (Measurement of current)
- Coulometry (Measurement of electricity)

Preparation of indicators

1.Acid base indicator

a) Methyl red ($C_{15}H_{15}N_{30}$)

Dissolve 0.5g of methyl red in 100 ml of 95% alcohol

b) Methyl orange ($C_{14}H_{15}N_3SO_4$)

- Free acid / sodium salt
- Dissolve 0.5g of free acid in 1000 ml of distilled water and filter
- Dissolve 0.5g of sodium salt in 1000 ml of distilled water + 15.2 ml of 0.1N HCl – filter

c) Phenolphthalein ($C_{20}H_{14}O_4$)

Dissolve 0.5 g of phenolphthalein in 100 ml of 95% alcohol

2.Mixed / Double indicator

Bromocresol green – Methyl red (Double indicator)

Dissolve 0.5 g of bromocresol green and 0.1g of methyl red in 100 ml of 95% ethanol and neutralize to mid colour (bluish purple)

3.Precipitometric indicators

Potassium chromate(K_2CrO_4)

Dissolve 5.0g of AR grade K_2CrO_4 in 100 ml of distilled water.

4.Redox indicators

Diphenylamine (C_6H_5-NH- C_6H_5)

Dissolve 0.5g of diphenylamine in 20 ml of H_2O + 100 ml of conc H_2SO_4

5.Complexometric indicators

Murexide

Grind 10g of NH_4Cl + 40 g of K_2SO_4 and 0.10 g Ammonium purpurate

Eriochrome Black T (EBT)

Dissolve 0.50g of of EBT and 4.5g of hydroxyl amine hydrochloride in 100 ml of 95% of alcohol.

Buffer Solutions

Buffer solution – Resist sudden change of pH due to addition of small amount acid (or) in base in a solution

Buffer added into a reaction — Solution pH remains almost same

Properties of a buffer

- Definite pH at a particular concentration
- pH should be practically unchanged if diluted
- pH should slightly change by addition of strong acid / strong base

Types of buffer solutions

1. Acidic
2. Alkaline
3. Ampholytes

1. Acidic buffer solutions

- Buffer solution — pH < 7
- Made from weak acid + its salt: Sodium salt

Example

$CH_3COOH + CH_3COONa$ (pH : 3.7-5.6)

2. Alkaline buffer solutions

- Buffer solution — pH > 7
- Made from weak base + its salt

Example

$NH_4OH + NH_4Cl$ (pH -9.35)

3. Ampholytes

- Amphoteric electrolytes
- Acting as both acid and base

Example

Glycine

CH_3-CH-COO^- + H^+
 |
 NH_2

(Acts as an acid)

CH_3-CH-COOH
 |
 NH_3+

(Act as base)

Mechanism of buffer action

A) Acidic buffer solutions

- Acetic acid (CH_3COOH) – weak acid
- Adding CH_3COONa to this adds lots of extra CH_3COO^-
- According to Le Chateliers principle – equilibrium shift to the left
- $CH_3COOH \longrightarrow CH_3COO^- + H^+$

- $CH_3COONa \longrightarrow CH_3COO^- + Na^+$
- Due to common ion effect (CH_3COO^-) the equilibrium turns towards the left
- Unionized form of CH_3COOH is formed
- Enough H^+ to make the solution acidic

Adding acid to the buffer system

- An acid is added to the buffer system
- H^+ will combine with $CH_3COO^- \longrightarrow CH_3COOH$
- Reverse reaction takes place and unionized form of CH_3COOH is formed

$$CH_3COOH \longrightarrow CH_3COO^- + H^+$$

$$HCl \longrightarrow H^+ + Cl^-$$

$$CH_3COOH \rightleftharpoons H^+ + CH_3COO^-$$

Adding alkali to the buffer system

- Alkaline solution contains OH

$$OH^- + CH_3COOH \longrightarrow CH_3COO^- + H_2O$$

$$CH_3COOH \longrightarrow H^+ + CH_3COO^-$$

$$NaOH \longrightarrow Na^+ + OH^-$$

$$H^+ + OH^- \longrightarrow H_2O$$

B) Alkaline buffer solutions

- Example: $NH_4OH + NH_4Cl$
- NH_4OH – weak base
- Adding NH_4Cl to NH_4OH — Extra NH_4^+
- According to Le Chateliers principle, the portion of the equilibrium shift to the left

$$NH_4OH \longrightarrow NH_4^+ + OH^-$$

$$NH_4Cl \longrightarrow NH_4^+ + Cl^-$$

$$NH_4OH \rightleftharpoons NH_4^+ + OH^-$$

- Lots of unreacted NH_4OH

- Lots of NH_4^+ from NH_4Cl
- $OH^- \longrightarrow$ Make the solution - alkaline

Adding acid to the buffer system

- Adding acid to a buffer system H^+ reacts with OH^- and form H_2O

$OH^- + H^+ \longrightarrow H_2O$

$NH_4OH \longrightarrow NH_4^+ + OH^-$

$NH_4Cl \longrightarrow NH_4^+ + Cl^-$

$HCl \longrightarrow H^+ + Cl^-$

$H^+ + OH^- \longrightarrow H_2O$

$NH_4^+ + Cl^- \longrightarrow NH_4Cl$

Adding alkali to the buffer system

Adding alkali to the buffer system, $OH^- + NH_4^+ \longrightarrow NH_3 + H_2O$

$NH_4OH \longrightarrow NH_4^+ + OH^-$

$NaOH \longrightarrow Na^+ + OH^-$

$NH_4^+ + OH^- \longrightarrow NH_4OH$

Henderson – Hasselbach equation

- Used to calculate the pH of a buffer solution from the initial concentration of the weak acid, and salt

$pH = 14 - pOH$

$pH = pKa + \log$

Preparation of buffer solutions

Sl.no	pH	Preparation
1	3	10.21g of potassium hydrogrn phthalate + 223 ml of 0.1M HCl
2	4	10.21g of potassium hydrogrn phthalate + 1 ml of 0.1M HCl
3	5	10.21g of potassium hydrogrn phthalate + 226 ml of 0.10M NaOH
4	6	6.81g of potassium hydrogen phthalate + 56 ml of 0.1M NaOH
5	7	6.81g of potassium phosphate monobasic + 291 ml of 0.1M NaOH
6	8	6.81g of potassium phosphate monobasic + 467 ml of 0.1M NaOH
7	9	4.77g of $Na_2B_4O_7$ + 46 ml of 0.1M HCl
8	10	4.77g of $Na_2B_4O_7$ + 183 ml of 0.1M NaOH
9	11	2.10g of $NaHCO_3$ + 227ml of 0.1M NaOH

- Each of the mixture is diluted to 1000 ml with distilled water
- pH of buffer must be checked and adjusted before being bottled
- If the pH is high — Adjust the pH by adding 1M HCl
- If the pH is low — Adjust the pH by adding 1M NaOH

Chapter 7

Theory of Acidimetry, Alkalimetry Oxidometry, Complexometry and Thiocyanaometry

Volumetry / Titrimetry

Process of determining the volume of solution of known concentration required to complete reaction with a solution of unknown concentration (test solution) by titration.

Example

0.1 N Na_2CO_3 – solution of known concentration

» 0.1 N HCl – solution of unknown concentration (Test solution)

Law of chemical equivalents

- Volumetric analysis – law of chemical equivalents
- $V_1N_1 = V_2N_2$

Classification of volumetric methods

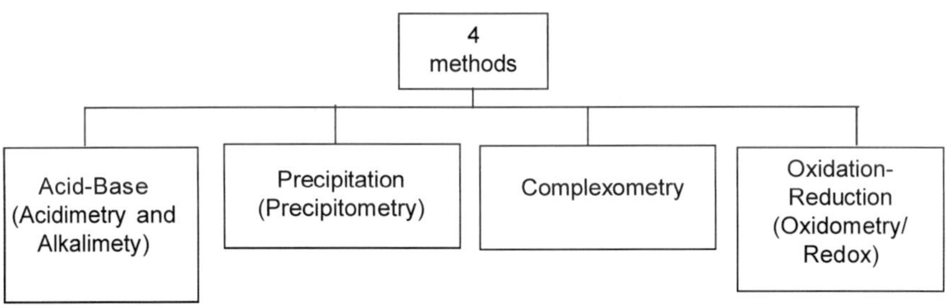

I. Acid –Base (Acidimetry and Alkalimetry)

- Neutralization reaction
- End point – using indicator

- Acidimetry – Determination of strength of an acid using standard alkali
- End point – easy to detect
- Colour change/ change in pH – pH meter

Acidimetry

Example – Na_2CO_3 vs. HCl

Alkalimetry

Example – $(CH_2COOH)_2$ vs. KOH

Arrhenius Theory

Acid – substance when dissolved in water gives H^+

$H_2SO_4 \rightarrow 2H^+ + SO_4^{2-}$ (strongly dissociated)

$HCl \rightarrow H^+ + Cl^-$ (strongly dissociated)

$CH_3COOH \rightarrow H^+ + CH_3COO^-$ (Poorly dissociated)

Base – substance when dissolved in water gives OH^-

$NaOH \rightarrow Na^+ + OH^-$ (strongly dissociated)

$Ca(OH)_2 \rightarrow Ca^{++} + 2OH^-$ (poorly dissociated)

$NH_4OH \rightarrow NH_4^+ + OH^-$ (Poorly dissociated)

- HCl - strongly dissociated - *strong acid*
- CH_3COOH - poorly dissociated - *weak acid*
- NaOH - strongly dissociated - *strong base*
- NH_4OH - poorly dissociated - *weak base*
- Acid - base titration – Neutralization reaction
- An acid is reacted with an equivalent amount of base
- Titrant – always strong acid/ strong base
- Analyte (titrate) – strong base/ strong acid/ weak acid / weak base

Common neutralization reaction

$HCl + NaOH \rightarrow NaCl + H_2O$

$H^+ + Cl^- + Na^+ + OH^-$

- pH of an acid is always < 7 and alkali > 7
- Point at which neutralization – End point
- Rate at which the H^+ is changed by the adding of acid / alkali
- If strong acid + strong base is used – abrupt change in H^+ at the end point
- Either acid/alkali are weak– change will not be abrupt – possible to locate the end point
- Acid + base – weak – change will be very gradual – can't locate the end point

Merits

Acid base reactions are very suitable for titrimetric analysis because

- Fast / rapid
- Free from side reaction
- Stoichiometric

II. Precipitation (Precipitiometry)

Titrant forms an insoluble product with an analyte

Example : Titartion of Cl^- with $AgNO_3 \rightarrow AgCl$

- Titartion – Sparingly soluble compunds (precipitates) are formed called precipitometry

Precipitaion reaction – Titrimetric analysis- conditions

1. Rate of reaction between the precipitant and the substance to be precipitated must be fast
2. Reaction should be stoichiometric
3. There should not be any co-precipitation
4. A suitable indicator should be available to locate the end point. Apart from visual indicator, the end point can also be identified by measuring some physical properties – electrical conductance/light scattering

Demerits

- Lack of suitable indicator
- Rate of reaction is too slow for a convenient titration
- Composition of the precipitates sometimes is not fixed due to co-precipitation so the stoichiometry of the reaction is not definite causing error

Precipitometry is carried out in 2 ways

1. Direct method (Mohr's Method) - Argentimetry

- Halide solution is taken in the titrate flask
- $AgNO_3$ – Burette
- Indicator – K_2CrO_4
- End point – Brick red (Ag_2CrO_4)
- Ag compounds – Argentimetry
- $NaCl + AgNO_3 \rightarrow NaNO_3 + AgCl$
- $2AgCl + K_2CrO_4 \rightarrow Ag_2CrO_4$ (Brick red ppt)$+ 2KCl$

2. Indirect method (Voltard's method) - Thiocyanometry

- If the halides are not neutral – Argentimetry is not possible
- $KSCN/NH_4SCN$ is used
- Indicator : Ferric alum
- End point : orange red colour
- Acid - prevent the hydrolysis of Fe^{3+}

  $AgNO_3 + KSCN \rightarrow AgSCN + KNO_3$

Demerits

It can't be employed if solution itself is strongly coloured

Example : Ca, Ni and Cu halides

- AgSCN has a strong tendency to absorb Ag^+ from the solution and hence the end point will be reached prematurely
- There are certain dyes which are strongly adsorbed by colloidal precipitates

- In a precipitation titration, the adsorption of indicators acts as a mean for locating the end point called adsorption indicators.

Example

- Sodium salt of fluoresceinate is used as an indicator in the titration of Cl with $AgNO_3$
- After the equivalence point, the indicator ions are adsorbed by the precipitate particles and becomes pink
- Colour change yellowish green → pink – End point

Application of precipitation reactions

To determine

- Ag and Cl
- Iodometry
- Oxidised form of halogens
- PO_4^{3-},ASO_4^{3-},CrO_4^{2-},MoO_4^{2-}
- Zn with $Fe(CN)_2$
- Pb with MoO_4

III. Complexometry

- Reaction involving complex formation- complexometry
- Titrant forms water soluble complexes with an analyte, metal ion
- Titrant – chelating agent
- EDTA- Ethylene Diamine Tetra Acetic Acid- most widely used chelating agent
- Indicators- To form a highly coloured complex with metal ion.

Chelating agents

An organic agent has two (or) more groups capable of complexing with a metal cation

- Complex- chelate
- Chelating agents: examples

  EDTA- Ethylene Diamine Tetra Acetic Acid

DTPA-Diethylene Triamine Penta Acetic Acid

NITA-Nitrilo Tri Acetic Acid

- DCTA – Diamino cyclohexane Tetra Acetic Acid
- EDTA- powerful complexing agent
- With several metal ions it forms stable five membered rings
- EDTA forms stable complex with Ca+Mg
- EDTA – to determine Zn^{2+}, Ba^{2+}, Cu^{2+}, Fe^{2+}
- EDTA titration –buffers
- Tartarate/citrate/ NH_4OH+NH_4Cl
- pH – 8-10

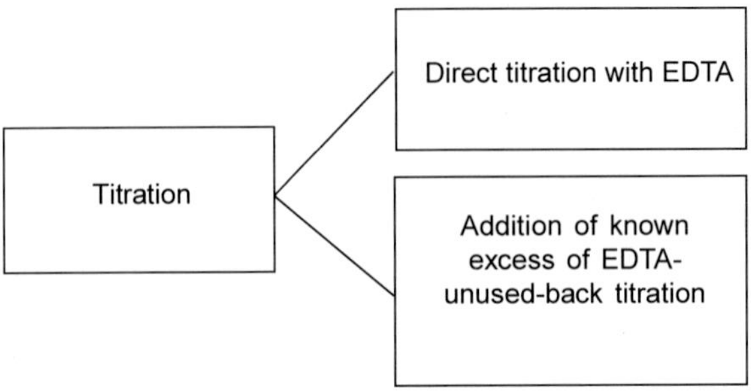

Complexometric estimation of Ca and Mg

- Ca^{2+} reacts with EDTA – stable complex
- Ca^{2+} reacts first – pH 12.0 by NaOH
- Indicator : Murexide
- Mg^{2+} - pH 10.0 buffer : NH_4Cl + NH_4OH
- Indicator : Erichrome Black T
- Ca-EDTA complex – more stable than Mg-EDTA
- Ca – indicator complex- less stable than Mg-indicator complex
- Titartion of EDTA with Ca^{2+} - A sharp end point – not observed
- Titration of EDTA with Mg^{2+} - A sharp end point - observed

Metallochromic indicator/Metal indicator

Indicator forms stable complex with metal ions

Example

Erichrome Black T - titration of Mg^{2+} with EDTA

(iv) Oxidation-Reduction (Oxidometry/Redox Titrimetry)

- Titration of oxidising agent with a reducing agent
- Oxidising agent gains electrons

Example

$KMnO_4$, $K_2Cr_2O_7$

- Reducing agent losses electrons

Example

- $FeSO_4(NH_4)_2SO_4\ 6H_2O$
- COOH
  |
  COOH
- Reactions in which electrons are transferred from one atom, ion (or) molecule to another is called Redox reactions
- Oxidation – Reduction titration : constituents under estimation is oxidised/reduced with the titrant
- Standard solution – oxidant is used in titration – oxidometric method

Example

$K_2Cr_2O_7$(Oxidant) $\rightarrow$ Standardise $FeSO_4$ (Reducing agent)

Oxidants and Reductants

(a). Oxidising agents (oxidant)

Substance gains electrons are reduced

Example

$KMnO_4$, $K_2Cr_2O_7$, KIO_3, $KBrO_3$, $CeSO_4$, I_2, PbO, $KHIO_3$

(b). Reducing agents (Reductants)

Substance which losses electrons and gets oxidised

Example

$FeSO_4$,$FeSO_4(NH_4)_2SO_4$,$(COOH)_2$,$(COONa)_2$, $Na_2S_2O_3$

Classification of redox titrimetry

- Permanganate titration (Permanganometry)
- Dichromate titration (Dichrometry)
- Iodometry
- Cuprimetry
- Bromometry
- Titanometry
- Vanadometry

(i) Permanganometry (Permanganate titration)

- $KMnO_4$ is an oxidising agent
- Reducing agents like $(COOH)_2$, Fe salts can be detrmined – permanganometry
- Oxidising power of $KMnO_4$ is greater in acidic medium
- Alkaline and neutral medium – MnO_2 is precipitated
- H_2SO_4 is used – Acidulating $KMnO_4$
- HNO_3, HCl – not used
- HNO_3 – oxidising agent
- HCl – oxidised by $KMnO_4$ – Cl_2 is formed

  $2KMnO_4 + 3H_2SO_4 \rightarrow K_2SO_4 + MnSO_4 + 3H_2O + 5(O)$

  $2FeSO_4 + H_2SO_4 + (O) \rightarrow Fe_2(SO_4)_3 + 5H_2O$

  $(COOH)_2 + O \rightarrow 2CO_2 + H_2O$

  Points to be remembered while employing $KMnO_4$

- $KMnO_4$ attacks all forms of organic matter including rubber tubes and filter papers
- $KMnO_4$ - decomposes on light
- Reactions with $KMnO_4$ is slow at room temperature and faster at 60-70°C
- Brown colouration may be formed due to cold reactants (or) rapid addition of $KMnO_4$ (or) presence of very little H_2SO_4. This is due to formation of MnO_2 – titration should be repeated fresh

- H_2SO_4 used should not contain NO_2 – decolourize $KMnO_4$
- To avoid brown stain of MnO_2 – glass wares should be cleaned immediately after using dil. $FeSO_4$ – to remove stain

(ii). Dichrometry (Dichrometric titrations)

- Redox estimation – $K_2Cr_2O_7$
- $K_2Cr_2O_7$ is less powerful than $KMnO_4$

Advantages of $K_2Cr_2O_7$

- Chemical is available in pure state – excellent primary standard
- Stable in solution/solid forms
- Doesn't oxidise HCl – (if not exceed 20%)
- Titration can be carried out – HCl/Cl
- Not attack rubber – measured by burette with rubber tap

Indicator used in Dichrometry

- Diphenyl amine, Diphenyl amine sulphonate
- $K_2Cr_2O_7$ – volumetric determination of Fe in the presence of dil HCl/H_2SO_4

  $K_2Cr_2O_7 + 4H_2SO_4 \rightarrow K_2SO_4 + Cr_2(SO_4)_3 + 4H_2O + 3(O)$

  $K_2Cr_2O_7 + 8HCl \rightarrow KCl + CrCl_3 + 4H_2O + 3(O)$

  $FeSO_4 + H_2SO_4 + (O) \rightarrow Fe_2(SO_4)_3 + H_2O$

(iii). Iodimetry and Iodometry (I_2 titrations)

(a) Iodimetry

- Volumetry involving I_2 solution directly for the estimation of reducing agents like thiosulphate, sulphites, arsenates
- Usually performed in neutral/alkaline (pH 8) to weakly acidic solution
- If the pH is too alkaline , I_2 will disproportionate into hypoiodallic and I
  - $I_2 + 2OH^- \rightarrow IO^- + I^- + H_2O$
  - $2Na_2S_2O_3 + I_2 \rightarrow Na_2S_4O_6 + 2NaI$
  - $Na_2SO_3 + I_2 \rightarrow Na_2SO_4 + 2HI$

(b). Iodometry

- Iodide salts liberate I_2 by the action of an oxidsing agent and the liberated I_2 is determined by a reducing agent
- It includes determination of oxidising agents like $KMnO_4$, $K_2Cr_2O_7$, $CuSO_4$ etc.
- When an excess of I_2 is added to a solution of an oxidising agent, I_2 is produced in amount equivalent to the oxidising agent present
- This I_2 is titrated against a reducing agent

  $2CuSO_4 + 4KI \rightarrow 2CuI + 2K_2SO_4 + I_2$

  $2Na_2S_2O_3 + I_2 \rightarrow Na_2S_4O_6 + 2NaI$
- Indicator : Starch
- End point : Disappearance of blue colour
- Indicator starch is not added at the beginning of titration when the I_2 concentartion is high.
- Starch is added just before end point when the dilute I_2 colour becomes pale yellow

Reason

i. I_2 - starch complex is only slowly dissociated and diffuse end point would result if large amount of I_2 were adsorbed on starch

ii. Most iodometric titrations are performed in strongly acid medium as the starch has a tendency to hydrolyse in acid solution

(iv) Cuprimetry

- Reducing sugars can be estimated by titration with Fehling solution where Cu^{++} - oxidising agent
- Cu^{++} salt in alkaline medium – reduced to Cu^{+} salt by glucose

CH_2OH

|

$CH_2OH + 2CuO \rightarrow (CHOH)_4 + Cu_2O$

|

$(CHOH)_4$

|

CHO

Plotting of titration curves

- Titration curve is constructed by plotting the pH of the solution as the function of the volume of titrant added
- When an acid is titrated against an alkali, the pH goes on increasing gradually
- At a certain point, a large change in pH is produced by even small addition of the alkali
- If a curve is plotted, it will be seen that for some distance the curve becomes almost parallel with the pH axis and then again tends away → Titration curve
- The region of abrupt change of titration curve → equivalence point
- The pH at equivalence point is 7, the titration is strong acid vs. strong base
- Equivalence point → pH < 7, → weak acid vs. strong base
- Weak acid vs. weak base – difficult to locate the equivalence point

(a) Strong acid vs. strong base

- Strong acid vs. strong base – both titrant and analyte- completely ionised

Example

- $HCl + NaOH \rightarrow NaCl + H_2O$
- $H^+ + OH^- \rightarrow H_2O$
- $Na^+, Cl^- \rightarrow$ remain unchanged
- Net result: Neutralization-NaCl
  - Salt NaCl – not hydrolyse – pH at equivalence point is 7
  - The titration exponent (pT) is the pH at which the titration in the presence of a given indicator.
  - Indicator with a titration exponent (pT) of 7.0 is suitable
  - Indicator with pH 4.0-10.0 can be used

Example

Methyl orange, Phenolphthalein

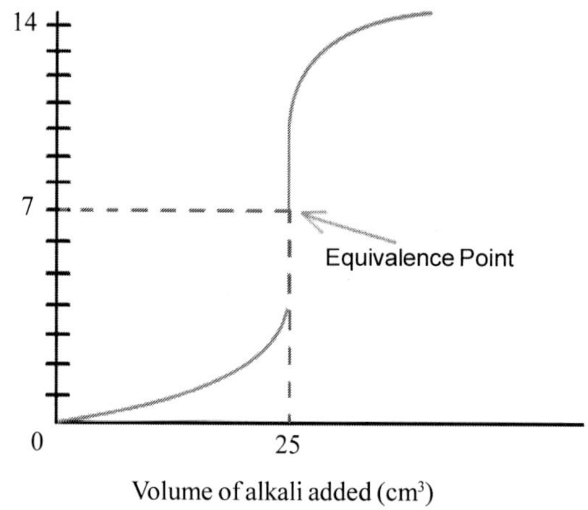

Fig. 1: Strong acid vs. Strong base titration curve

(b). Weak acid vs. strong base

$CH_3COOH + NaOH \rightarrow CH_3COONa + H_2O$

- CH_3COOH – weak acid $\rightarrow$ poorly dissociated
- NaOH – strong base $\rightarrow$ strongly dissociated
- Resultant solution – alkaline
- Equivalence point: $p^H > 7$
- Region of change is between pH 7.73 and 10.0
- Phenolphthalein $\rightarrow$ Best indicator

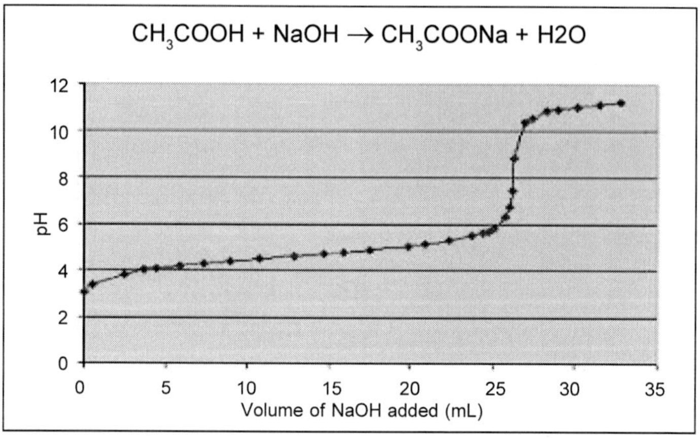

Fig. 2: Weak acid vs. strong base titration curve

(c). Strong acid vs. weak base

$HCl + NH_4OH \rightarrow NH_4Cl + H_2O$

- NH_4OH – poorly dissociated
- Resultant solution – acidic
- Equivalence point – acidic range (pH 5.12)
- Region of abrupt change is 4 and 6.2
- Suitable indicator : Methyl red, Methyl orange

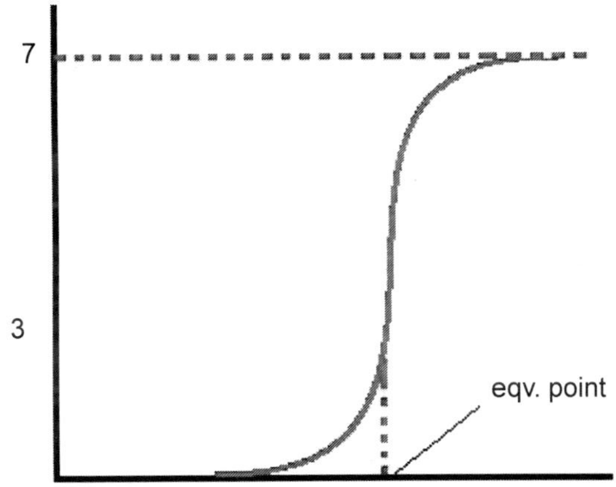

Fig. 3: Strong acid vs. weak base titration curve

(d). Weak acid vs. weak base

$CH_3COOH + NH_4OH$ ® $CH_3COONH_4 + H_2O$

- No pH break
- Titration can't be performed accurately with any of known indicators
- Therefore in neutralization titration – one reacting substance must be a strong electrolyte

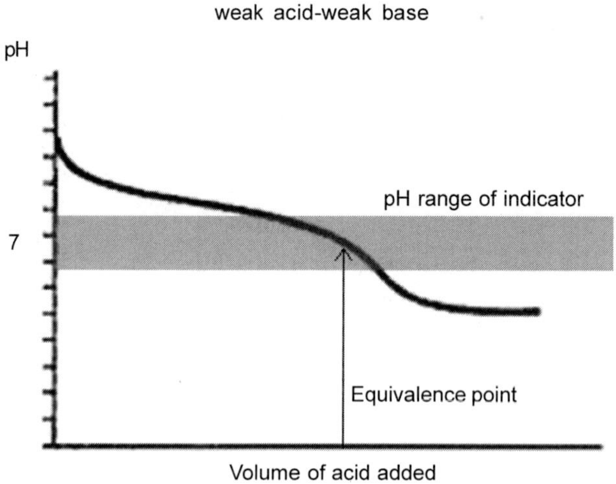

Fig. 4: Weak acid vs. weak base titration curve

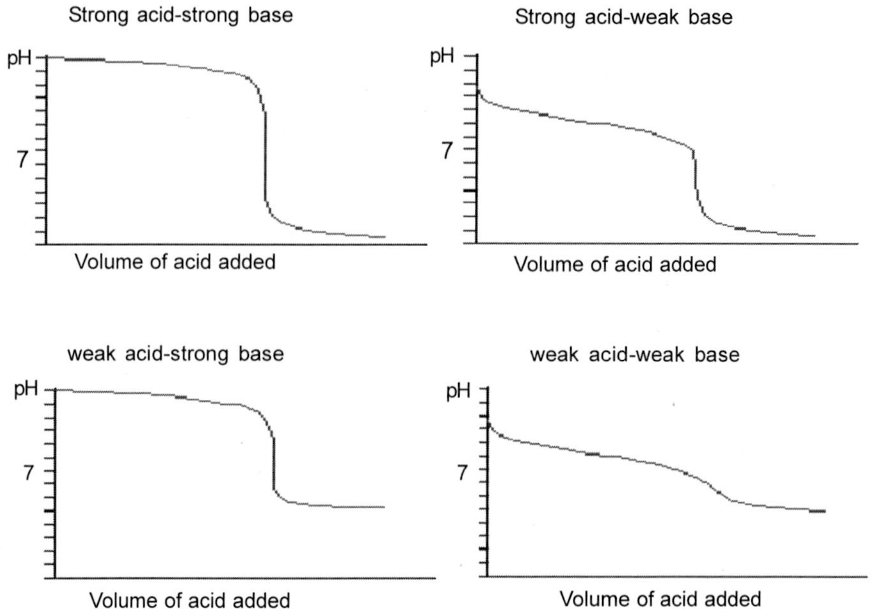

Fig. 5: Titration curves

Chapter 8

Gravimetric Analysis Principles and Techniques

Gravimetric analysis

Techniques – analyte is determined by quantitative isolation of substance by precipitation and weighing the precipitate

Example

NaCl – precipitating agent (precipitant)

AgCl – precipitate

Principle

2 methods

Precipitation	Volatilization

Precipitation

- Constituent is isolated from the substance by forming an insoluble precipitate

Volatilization

- Analyte is volatilized and loss in weight is determined.

Pre requisite for gravimetric analysis

- Ion being determined must be completely precipitated
- Precipitate must be pure stable compound of definite chemical composition

- Precipitate must be easily filtered
- Precipitate – insoluble – no appreciable loss during filtration
- Very insoluble precipitates are not best for gravimetric analysis

  Example: $Fe(OH)_2$
- Must be coarse granular
- Size of the particle should be large enough not to pass through the filter paper
- Weighable form should be stable for a longer time.

A) Precipitation Method

Steps involved in gravimetric analysis

I) Precipitation of the solution

- Adjustment of the pH of a solution to favour precipitation, removal of interferences adjusting the volume of the sample to suit the amount of precipitating agent

Example

In the analysis of Ca, $(COOCa)_2$ precipitate is soluble in basic medium, but at low pH

COO^- combines with H^+ – weak acid

II)Precipitation

- Addition of precipitating agent to the sample solution

Steps involved

1. *Super saturation*: The solution phase contains more of dissolved salts than at equilibrium
2. *Nucleation* : Small number of ions, atoms and molecules come together to produce a microscopic nuclei
3. *Particle growth*: Particles grown three dimensionally with the addition of ions of the precipitates to form a larger crystal.

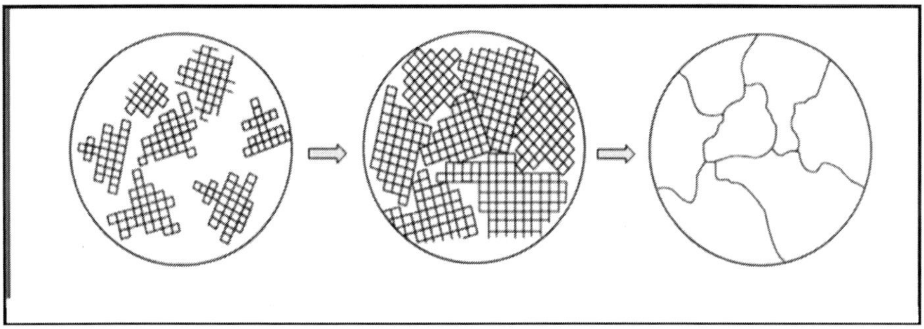

Von Weiman proposed the Relative super saturation (RSS) formula

$$\text{Relative super saturation} = \frac{Q - S}{S}$$

Where Q= concentration of the reactants before precipitation (or) the degree of super saturation

S= solubility of the precipitate at equilibrium

III) Digestion of the precipitate

- When the precipitate is hot and allowed to stand in the presence of mother liquor for 30 minutes to 1 hour, dissolution of smaller crystal occur and growth of larger crystal takes place called Digestion or Ostwald ripening

  Digestion – small colloidal particles – Agglomerate – surface area decreases and adsorption

- Colloidal particles tend to absorb its own ions present in excess forming primary ion layer – attracts ions form solution – secondary ion/ counter ion layer.

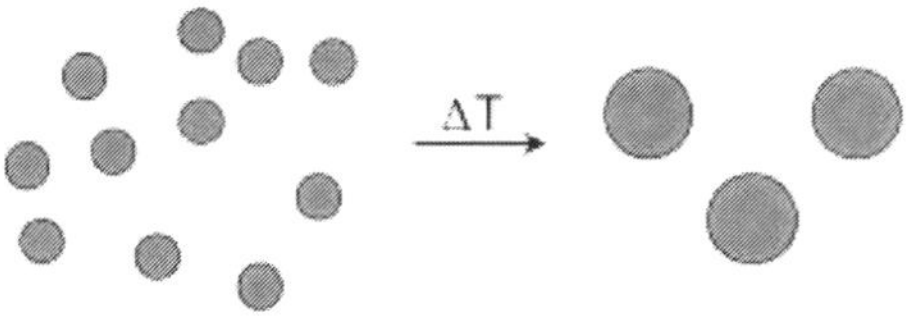

IV) Washing and filtration

- Washing – To move the co precipitate impurities, absorbed species and the mother liquor
- Many precipitates cannot be washed with pure water and part of the precipitate may be lost and peptization may occur in colloidal precipitates.

Peptization

- Reverse of coagulation, caused by the entry of the molecules between the primary and secondary layer and particle revert to colloidal state.
- To avoid peptization- Dil. HNO_3, NH_4NO_3, Dil CH_3COOH are added

Filtration

- Done by Gooch/ignition filter paper
- To test completion of washing, few drops of the filtrate is collected and checked for the presence of precipitating agent.

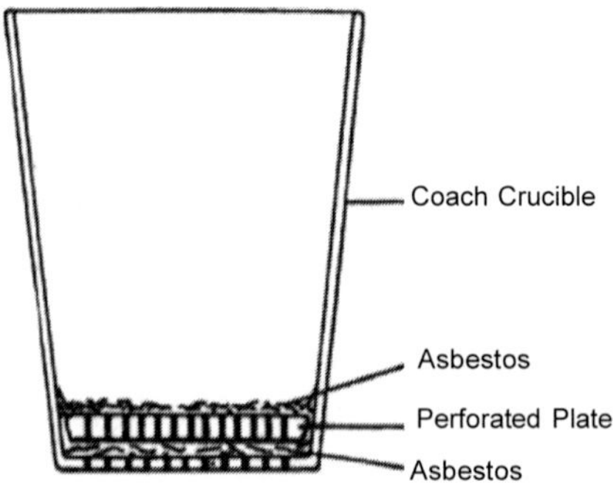

Gooch Crucible

V) Drying and ignition

- Precipitate is dried at 110 -120°C for 1-2 hours to remove water and adsorbed precipitates
- Ignition in a muffle furnace at temperature ranging from 600-1200°C to get a material with exactly known chemical structure.

Impurities in precipitates

Precipitates carry other constituents normally – soluble – contamination or co-precipitation

Co- precipitation occurs by

a. Occlusion
b. Inclusion
c. Surface adsorption
d. Isomorphous replacement
e. Post precipitation

a) Occlusion

- H_2O, analyte ions, precipitating agent ions get trapped in the crystal structure causing occlusion
- Occlusion can be avoided by slow addition of precipitating agent

b) Inclusion

- Occurs when ions of similar size and charges are trapped within the crystal lattice
- Purification by dissolving and reprecipitation

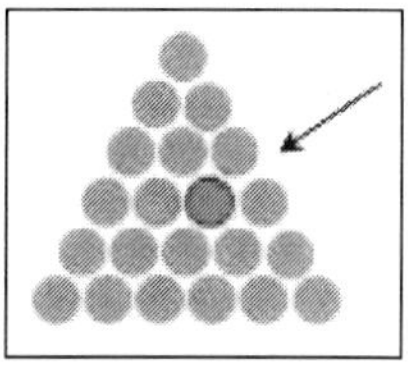

Example

K^+ in NH_4MgPO_4 precipitate

Ionic radii of K^+ - 1.33 A°

NH_4^+ - 1.48 A°

c) Surface adsorption

- Common source of ions is gelatinous precipitates
- Due to the primary adsorbed layer of the lattice ions
- Can be reduced by proper digestion and washing.

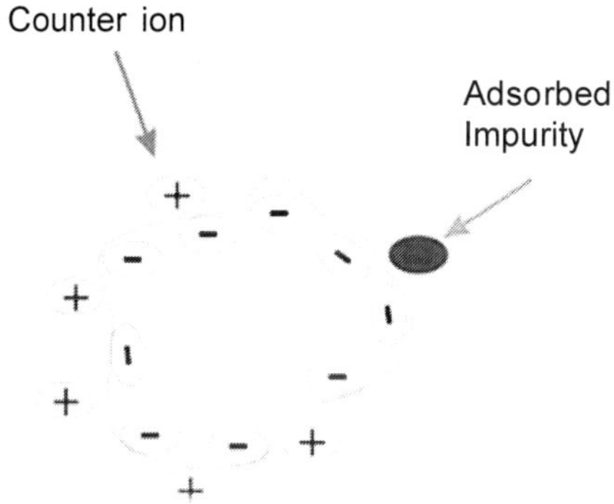

d) Isomorphous replacement

- Replacement of one ion by the other having similar ionic radii/ lattice dimension – mixed crystal.

Example

In the precipitates of Magnesium ammonium phosphate, K^+ replaces NH_4^+ and form Magnesium potassium phosphate.

e) Post precipitation

- When the precipitate is allowed to stand in contact with the mother liquor for a longer time, ions other than the analyte forms precipitate over the original precipitate.

Example

In the precipitate of CuS in the presence of Zn, if not filtered, ZnS starts to precipitate on the top of it.

B) Volatilization Method

Method I

a) A sample is heated, volatile component is lost, trapped and the weight increase of the trap is measured

Example

Water collected in desiccant

b) Moisture content is determined by indirect method, weighed sample containing moisture is ignited and moisture bottle is weighed.

Example

Gravimetric estimation of moisture in moisture bottle.

Method II

- A sample is heated, the volatile component is collected , the weight loss of analyte is measured

Example

Determination of CO_3 inwhich sample is heated and CO_2 liberated is collected in NaOH solution forming Na_2CO_3

$$2\,NaOH + CO_2 \rightarrow Na_2CO_3 + H_2O$$

Features of gravimetric analysis

- Relative slow method
- Minimal requirement of equipments
- No calibration is required
- Results are based on formula weight

- Accuracy 1-2 parts per thousand (ppt)
- Useful if the analyte concentration of the sample is more than 1%.

Chapter 9

Precipitation, Solubility Product, Common Ion Effect and Conditions of Precipitation

Precipitation

- An ionic phenomena wherein the product of the ionic concentrations of a substance in a solution exceeds the solubility product
- Precipitate is often ignited before weighing to convert it into substance of definite chemical composition and chemical stability
- Compound precipitated — precipitated form

  Example: Magnesium ammonium phosphate
- When it is ignited — weighable form

  Example: $BaSO_4$

Precipitated form

- Low solubility
- Structure of the precipitate allows rapid filtration and washing
- Must be easily converted into weighable form

Weighable form

- Composition corresponds to the chemical formula
- Adequate chemical stability
- Content of the element determined should be very low

Precision in gravimetric analysis depends on

- Choice of precipitant: The precipitant used decide the properties of the precipitate

- Volatile
- Must be specific in its action
- Amount of precipitant
- Condition of precipitation

Precipitation equilibrium

a) Solubility in pure water

The equilibrium is straight forward and the precipitation occurs when ionic products just exceeds Ksp

Example 1

$AgCl_{(s)} \longrightarrow Ag^{+}_{(aq)} + Cl^{-}_{(aq)}$

When ionic product is greater the Ksp = 1.1×10^{-10}M precipitation occurs

$$[Ag^{+}][Cl^{-}] = 1.0\times10^{-10}M$$

$$[Ag^{+}]=[Cl^{-}] = 1.0\times10^{-5}M$$

Example 2

$PbSO_4(s) \longrightarrow Pb^{2+}_{(aq)} + SO_4^{2-}{}_{(aq)}$

At equilibrium

$$[Pb^{2+}]\,[SO_4^{2-}] = 1.6 \text{ X } 10^{-8}M$$

$$[Pb^{2+}] = [SO_4^{2-}] = 1.3 \text{ X } 10^{-4}\,M$$

b) Solubility in the presence of common ion

- Common ion added shifts the equilibrium to the left and decrease in solubility according to Le Chatelier principle

Example

Decrease in solubility of AgCl due to the addition of Ag — common ion

c) Solubility in the presence of diverse ions

- Diverse ions have a screening effect on dissociated ion which leads to extra dissocialtion
- Solubility will increase in the presence of diverse ions and the equilibrium will be towards right

Example: Solubility of AgCl in $NaNO_3$ solution

Conditions of precipitation

- Proper precipitating solution – pure precipitate + desirable properties
- Precipitating agent should be added drop by drop → solution does not become supersaturated
- Solution should be constantly stirred during the addition of precipitant
- A hot or a solution at the same temperature should be added to boiling solution → to set maximum solubility and minimum surface energy
- Precipitation should be carried out in dilute solution
- Precipitate must be insoluble in the mother liquor and in the wash liquid
- Precipitating agent should be added in slight excess only to complete the precipitation but not in great excess
- Orderly addition of reagents helps in the formation of coarse precipitate with definite chemical composition
- In crystalline precipitates, keeping them overnight with the mother liquor would decrease errors due to coprecipitation and give good readily filterable precipitate
- Precipitate should easily be separable from solution by filtration and should be easily washed free of soluble impurities
- Size of the particle should be large enough to prevent their passage through the filter paper
- Precipitates formed should be washed with dilute solutions of an electrolyte — precipitates has least solubility and colloids formation is prevented
- Precipitates should be capable to convert into granules/crystals of definite composition either by evaporation or by ignition
- Ageing helps in reducing the irregular surface to further deposition and dissolution and redeposition causing reduction in surface and also adsorption
- Elevated temperature favours particle growth
- Addition of volatile electrolytes induces flocculation

Solubility product

Defined as the product of the ionic concentration (moles/litre) of a slightly soluble salt in a saturated solution each raised to the power of its coefficient at a specific temperature.

It is represented as Ksp

Example 1

AgCl ——— is a strong electrolyte ionized into $Ag^+ + Cl^-$

$$AgCl \longrightarrow Ag^+ + Cl^-$$

$$(solid) \longrightarrow (solution)$$

- Equilibrium constant of these reaction is

$$Ksp = \frac{[Ag^+]\,[Cl^-]}{[AgCl]} \qquad (1)$$

The $[Ag^+]$ and $[Cl^-]$ → represents the concentrations of Ag^+ and Cl^- (moles/l)

- When the solution at equilibrium, the concentration of [AgCl] is a constant and from equation (1)

$[Ag^+]\,[Cl^-]$ = Keq x [AgCl]

= Keq x constant

= Ksp

Ksp of AgCl is 1.0×10^{-6} mole/litre

Example 2

$$Ag_2CrO_4 \longrightarrow 2Ag^+ + CrO_4^{2-}$$

$Ksp = [Ag^{2+}]\,[CrO_4^{2-}]$

Ksp of Ag_2CrO_4 is 1.12×10^{-12} moles/litre

Example 3

$$NaCl_{(solid)} \longrightarrow Na^+ + Cl^-$$

$Ksp = [Na^+]\,[Cl^-]$

Ksp of NaCl = 36 moles/litre

Solubility product and solubility

- Let us consider a saturated solution of AgCl in water

  $AgCl_{(s)} + H_2O \longrightarrow Ag^+_{(aq)} + Cl^-_{(aq)}$

- AgCl is a 1:1 salt, the concentration of Ag^+ and Cl^- in this solution are equal
- In a saturated solution of AgCl in water $[Ag^+] = [Cl^-]$

Adding Ag^+ to the solution

- When a few crystals of solid $AgNO_3$ are added to the saturated solution of AgCl in water, according to the solubility rules
- $AgNO_3$ is a soluble salt and dissolved and dissociated into Ag^+ and NO^-_3
- As a result, two sources of Ag^+ in this solution

  $AgNO_3(s) + H_2O \longrightarrow Ag^+_{(aq)} + NO^-_{(aq)}$

- There is an increase in Ag^+ concentration
- The solution is no longer at equilibrium because the product of the concentration of the Ag^+ and Cl^- is too large
- So the ionic product (Qsp) for the solution is larger than the solubility product (Ksp) for AgCl

  $Qsp = (Ag^+) + (Cl^-) > Ksp$

- Ionic product is the product of the concentrations of the ions at any moment of time
- When ionic product = solubility product – equilibrium
- There are two sources of Ag^+ in this solution, there will be more Ag^+ at equilibrium than Cl^-
- Saturated solution of AgCl to which $AgNO_3$ is added

  $[Ag^+] > [Cl^-]$

Addition of Cl^- to the solution

- When a few crystals of NaCl is added to a saturated solution of AgCl
- There are two sources of Cl^-

$NaCl_{(s)} \longrightarrow Na^{+} + Cl^{-}$

$AgCl_{(s)} \longrightarrow Ag^{+}_{(aq)} + Cl^{-}_{(aq)}$

- Ionic product is larger than the solubility product

  $Qsp = (Ag^{+}) + (Cl^{-}) > Ksp$

- When the reaction comes back to equilibrium, there will be more Cl^{-} in the solution than Ag^{+}
- Saturated solution of AgCl to which NaCl has been added

  $[Ag^{+}] > [Cl^{-}]$

Common ion effect

- Suppression of ionization of a weak electrolyte in a solution of strong electrolyte containing one of the ions as the weak electrolyte is called common ion effect
- According to Lechatlier's principle, if a system in equilibrium is subjected to stress the equilibrium will shift in the direction which tends to relieve the stress
- A salt is less soluble in solution containing an ion which is the same as one of its constituents. This is called as common ion effect.

Example 1

- To the solution of a weak acid / weak base, an electrolyte having a common ion is added the ionization of a weak acid / weak base is further suppressed
- If CH_3COONa is added to CH_3COOH, ionization of CH_3COOH decreased

  $CH_3COOH \longrightarrow H^{+} + CH_3COO^{-}$

  $CH_3COONa \longrightarrow Na^{+} + CH_3COO^{-}$

  $CH_3COOH \longrightarrow H^{+} + CH_3COO^{-}$

- If NH_4Cl is added to NH_4OH, ionization of NH_4OH decreases

  $NH_4OH \longrightarrow NH_4^{+} + OH^{-}$

  $NH_4Cl \longrightarrow NH_4^{+} + Cl^{-}$

  $NH_4OH \rightleftharpoons NH_4^{+} + OH^{-}$

Example 2

$AgCl_{(s)} \longrightarrow Ag^{+}_{(aq)} + Cl^{-}_{(aq)}$

- When $AgNO_3$ is added (common ion Ag^+), with the precipitate of AgCl
- Cl^- combine with Ag^+ and form AgCl
- More of AgCl precipitate is formed and decreasing solubility and Ksp will be constant

$AgCl \longrightarrow Ag^+ + Cl^-$

$NH_4Cl \longrightarrow NH_4^+ + Cl^-$

Diversion effect

Solubility of slightly soluble salt is increased in the presence of increased concentrations of certain salts without common ion $\longrightarrow$ Diversion effect / Neutral salt effect

Example

AgCl is more soluble in KNO_3 solution than in water

Ripening of the precipitate

- After precipitation, the precipitate is allowed to stand in the mother liquid for 2 to 24 hours $\longrightarrow$ Ripening
- This process promote aging which includes all irreversible structural changes in the precipitate after formation
- Ripening is carried out at elevated temperature and allowed to stand for overnight

Process of aging (Oswald's ripening of impurities)

- Re crystallization of primary particles
- Cementing of smaller crystals into larger crystals
- Growth of larger particles by dissolution of smaller particles and re precipitation on the surface of large crystals
- Thermal agitation of ions helps to form perfect structures
- Adsorbed or trapped impurities go into the solution
- Transformation of less stable forms into more stable forms

Types of impurities

- Two types
    I. Adsorbed impurities
    II. Co-precipitated impurities

I) Adsorbed impurities

- Impurities of the ions adsorbed themselves on the surface of the precipitate
- Impurities can be removed by washing

II) Co-precipitated impurities

- Precipitate of extraneous substances formed along with the main precipitates
- Cannot be removed by washing
- Can be reduced by adjusting the temperature, rate of addition of precipitant, sequence of addition of reagents, reprecipitation etc.

Chapter 10

Filtration – Choice of Filters and Washing Techniques

I. Filtration

Filtration is a process of separation of precipitate from solution. Filtration is used to remove impurities from a solution (or) to isolate a solid.

Types of filtration

2 types

Gravity filtration   Vacuum (or) suction filtration

(A) Gravity filtration

This method of filtration is used to remove solid impurities from an organic liquid due to gravitational force.

Procedure for standard gravity filtration

(i) Selection and folding of filter paper

While folding the filter paper, the size of the filter paper should be few millimeters below the rim of the glass funnel. The paper to be folded into a cone by first folding into half and then into half again.

(ii) The glass funnel is supported in a ring (or) placed in the neck of an Erlenmeyer flask (Conical flask). First the filter paper should be moistened with a few milliliters of solvent to be used for wetting the paper. Then the mixture to be filtered is poured through the funnel in portions. Fluted filter paper is better for gravity filtration with organic solvents.

Gravity Filtration

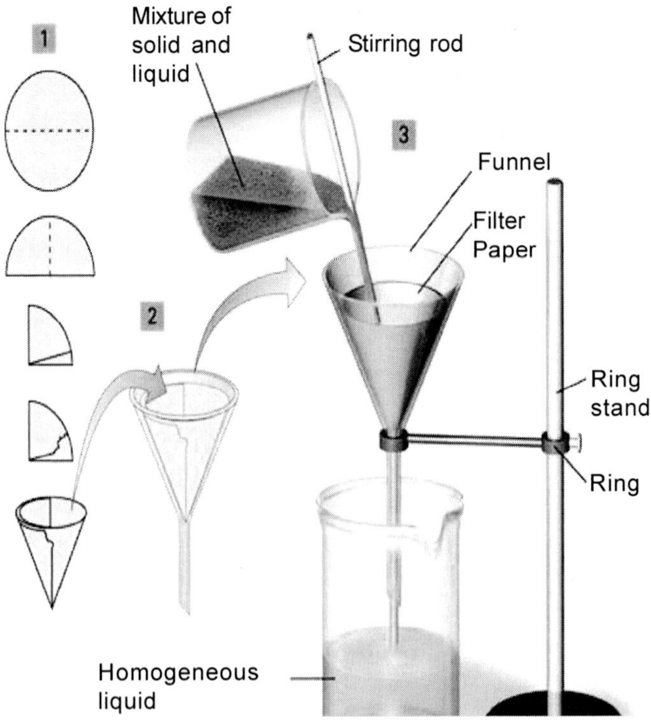

(B) Vacuum filtration

This method of filtration is used to collect desired solids viz., collection of crystals in a re-crystallization procedure. Buchner (or) Hirsch funnel is used in vacuum filtration. Vacuum filtration is faster than gravity filtration, because the solvent (or) solution and air is forced through filter paper by the application of pressure. This vacuum filtration should not be used to filter a solid from a liquid, if the liquid is low boiling.

Procedure for vacuum filtration

(i) Assembling the apparatus

The side arm of flask is checked carefully for cracks, since cracks could cause the flask to break while applying the vacuum. Then the flask is clamped securely to a ring stand. Over the flask an adapter and a Buchner funnel to be fitted. A piece of filter paper is placed in the funnel and the filter paper should cover all the holes in the filter.

(ii) The paper is moistened with a small amount of the solvent to be used in the filtration and the vacuum source is turned on.

(iii) The mixture to be filtered is poured onto the filter paper. The vacuum should rapidly pull the liquid through the funnel.

(iv) Vacuum pulls the solvent through the filter and into the filter flask.

(v) The cake is to be rinsed with a small amount of fresh, cold solvents to remove the impurities that are dissolved in the filtrate. The rubber tubing is disconnected before turning off the water aspiration. Then the filter paper is removed and the solid is collected.

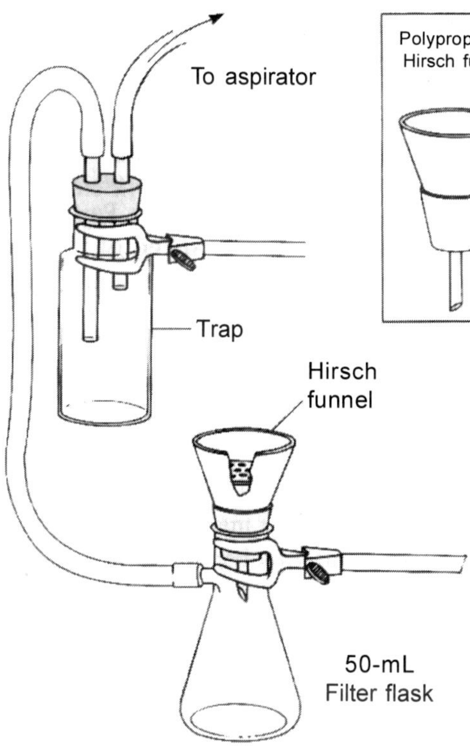

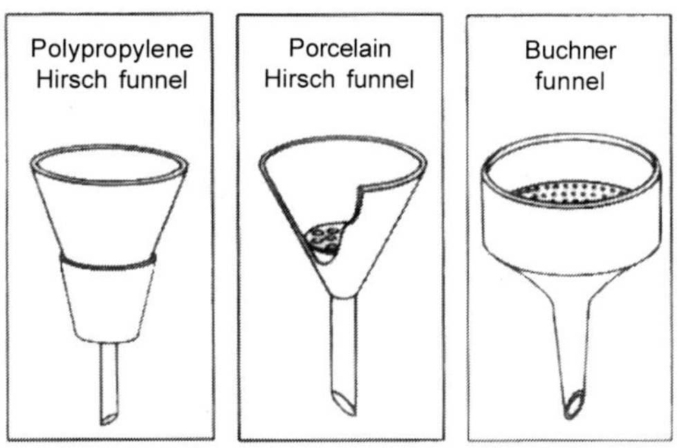

Steps in filtration

There are 3 basic steps in filtration.

a. Decantation

b. Washing

c. Transfer

(a) Decantation

It is the process of gently pouring off the liquid and leaving the precipitate undisturbed. The pores of any filtering medium will be clogged with the precipitate. The longer the transfer of precipitate can be delayed, the more rapid will be the freedom from impurity. The washings of the precipitate is carried out before it is transferred to the filter paper.

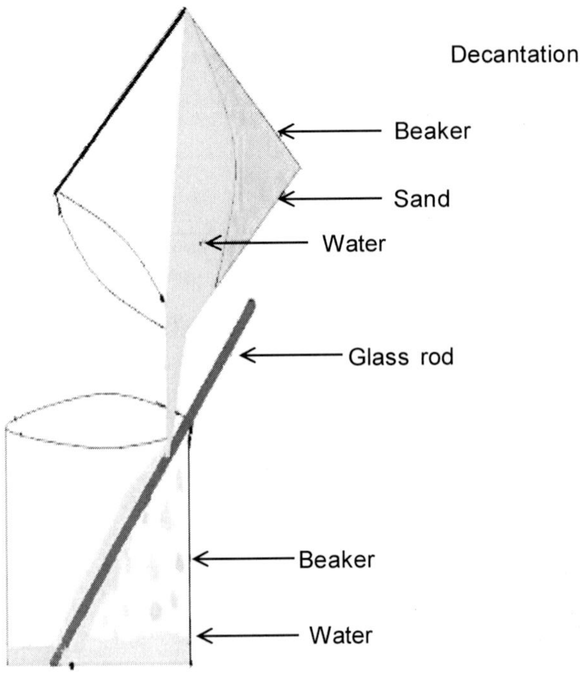

Creeping

Many precipitates have the property of spreading over the wetted surfaces against the force of gravity called as creeping. The filter should not be filled more than three quarters at a time.

(b) Washing

Washing of the precipitate should be done by adding small volume of wash liquid at a time. This is more effective in removing the soluble contaminants than adding total volume in one washing.

(c) Transfer

More precipitates should be retained in the filter paper. Use hot liquids for washing if solubility of precipitate is not affected, since hot liquid will hasten the rate of filtration.

Choice of filtering media

The choice of filtering medium depends on

- Size of the particle
- Ease of filtration
- Time of treatment of the precipitate

The commonly used filtering media are,

a) Filter paper

b) Thin pads of asbestos (used in Gooch)

c) Glass mating (used in Gooch)

d) Sintered glass

e) Glass wool

f) Muslin cloth

g) Filter crucibles

a) Filter paper

In gravimetric analysis special type of filter papers which have been treated with HCl (or) HF to remove the mineral substances like $CaCO_3$, SiO_3 etc. so that they can be ignited without a measurable residual ash. The choice of filter paper depends on the nature of the precipitate to be filtered.

Whatman filter papers

- Whatman No.40 – It is used for coarse crystalline precipitation like $(COO)_2Ca$, ammonium phospho molybdate, AgCl having medium speed of filtration. It retains 20-25 μm particles
- Whatman No.41 – It is very fast but due to open texture, it is not recommended for fine precipitates. It is used for gelatinous precipitate like $Ag(OH)_3$
- Whatman No.42 – It is of close texture and can be used for fine precipitates like $BaSO_4$, $MgNH_4PO_4$, etc.
- Whatman No.3 – It is having medium porosity with retention of 6 μm particles
- Whatman No.1 – It is used for qualitative work when ash weight of the paper is of no consequence.

Precipitate	Whatman filter papers
Very fine (Eg. $BaSO_4$)	No. 42 (2.5 mm)
Small (or)medium (Eg.AgCl)	No. 40 (8 mm)
Gelatinous (or) large crystals	No. 41 (20 – 25 mm)

Important points on using filter paper

- Cone of filter should be equal to funnel size. Correct filter paper should be selected ie., size of the filter paper depends on weight of the precipitates but not on volume of solution.
- It should be folded on its diameter and again folded to quarters. It is then opened upto form a cone with three folds on one side and fourth on the other side.
- Place the filter paper on a funnel, moistened with water and pressed to avoid air bubbles formed between filter paper and side of funnel.
- Funnel angle should be 60° with the stem length 5 cm to ensure rapid filtration.
- Edge of filter paper should be 1 cm below the rim.
- Clogging of pores of gelatinous precipitates like $Al(OH)_3$ or $Fe(OH)_3$ can be avoided by adding filter paper pulp. Pulp is prepared by boiling filter paper with concentrated HCl to disintegrate and wash with distilled water.

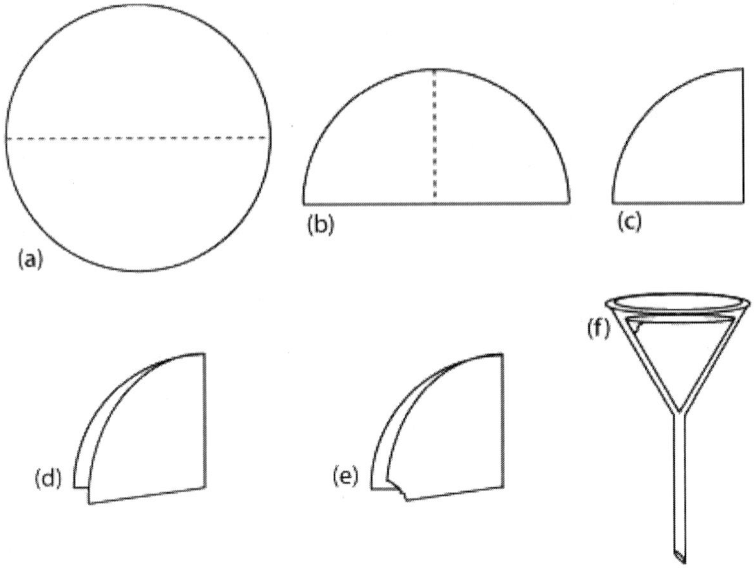

(b) Asbestos

A thin layer of asbestos fibres deposited on the perforated bottom of a porcelain crucible as a mat and used as filtering medium is called Gooch crucible. It provides an ideal filtering vessel for those precipitates, which are not ignited before weighing. Filtration is done by suction of an aqueous suspension of material through small holes in the bottom of crucible. The asbestos is inconvenient and potentially hazardous.

(c) Glass mat

It is available commercially and used in the bottom of a Gooch crucible instead of asbestos pad. They can tolerate temperature upto 500°C

(d) Sintered glass

The sintered glass crucible contains a sintered glass bottom which is available in fine, medium (or) coarse porosity. They can be used upto 500°C. These crucibles have sintered plate of different degrees of porosity to suit precipitates of different sizes. They are resistant to concentrated acids and most of the reagents. Glass filters are not recommended for concentrated alkali solutions because of possibility of attack by these solutions.

(e) Porcelain filter crucible

The porcelain filter crucible contains a porous unglazed bottom. Gelatinous precipitates such as $Fe(OH)_3$ should not be filtered in filter crucibles because they clog the pores. Filter crucibles are used with a crucible holder mounted on a filtering flask.

(f) Glass wool

It is used in the estimation of Fe by permanganometry.

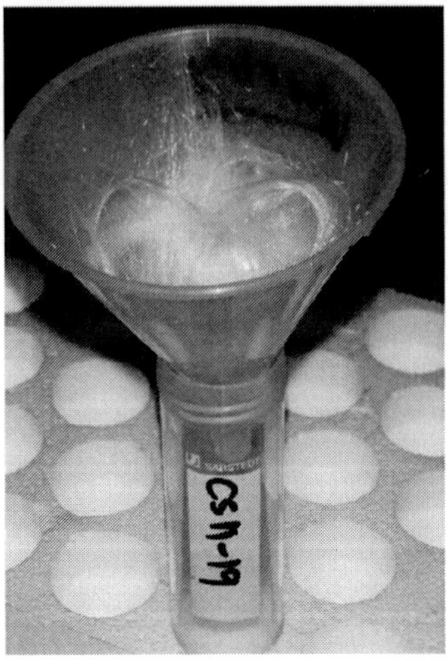

(g) Muslin cloth

It is used in crude fibre analysis.

II. Washing

The precipitate must be washed free of all soluble matters. Otherwise, impurities will remain sticking to the precipitate and on drying may cause error (or) may be added to gelatinous precipitate.

Hot liquids should be used for washing if solubility of precipitate is not affected because hot liquids will speed up filtration.

Types of wash solutions

1. Solutions which prevent the precipitate from becoming colloidal and passing through the filter

This property is observed with gelatinous (or) flocculated precipitates. A solution of an electrolyte like ammonium salts is used for washing such precipitates.

2. Solutions which reduce the solubility of precipitates

If the wash solution has an ion common to an ion in the precipitates, then the solubility of precipitate will be less in the wash solution

Example

Dilute $(COONH_4)_2$ solution is used for washing $(COO)_2Ca$

Organic solvents like C_2H_5OH and CH_3-O-CH_3 may be used for washing.

3. Solutions which prevent hydrolysis of salts of weak acids and bases

A precipitate of a salt of weak acid has a tendency to hydrolyse and product of such hydrolysis will be a base. So the wash liquid must be basic.

Example

$MgNH_4PO_4$ hydrolyse to give acid phosphate ion HPO_4^{2-} and hydroxide and therefore it should be washed with dilute NH_3 solution.

Steps for better granulation

- Addition of HNO_3 (or) NH_4NO_3
- Bringing $HCl/HNO_3/CH_3COOH$ medium to suppress the precipitation of other group metals.
- Stirring the solution with glass rod to hasten the precipitate formation.
- Thermostating (or) keeping over night for better granulation and also prevent colloidal formation

Ideal characteristics of a wash liquid

- The wash liquid should not solubilize precipitate but dissolve impurities easily.
- It should not have any dispersive active action on the precipitate
- It should not form volatile (or) insoluble product with the precipitate
- It should be easily volatilized at the temperature of drying of the precipitate.
- It should not contain any substance which may interfere with the determination of the constituents.

Chapter 11

Principles and Practices of Potentiometry and Conductometry

Potentiometry

Potentiometry is based on measurement of potential of an electrode system

Principle

When a metal electrode is immersed in a solution containing its own ions, the metal atom pass into the solution in the form of metal ions and a potential difference is established between the metal and the solution. This potential is called as electrode potential.

Potential on an electrode depends on the ions present in solution and their concentration which can be determined by using electrochemical cells and expressed by Nernst equation

$$M^{n+} + n_e \rightleftarrows \mathrm{M}$$

$$E = E_o - \frac{RT}{nF} ln \frac{1}{{}^{a}m^{n+}}$$

(or)

$$E_o - \frac{RT}{nF} \ln {}^{a} M^{a+}$$

Where

R = Gas constant

T = Absolute temperature

F = Faradays constant

n = Valency of the ion

${}^{a}M^{n+}$ = The activity of the ions in the solution

E = Electrode potential

Eo = Constant standard E.M. F depending upon the metal

Measurement of pH

pH is defined as the negative logarithm of H^+ activity at 25°C.

pH = - log (H^+)

$$= log \frac{1}{(H^+)}$$

= log 1 – log (H^+)

Principle

A glass electrode in contact with the H^+ of the solution acquires an electrode potential (E) which depends on the concentration of H^+. This is measured potentiometrically against a reference electrode. The potential difference between the glass electrode and reference electrode is expressed as pH.

pH meter

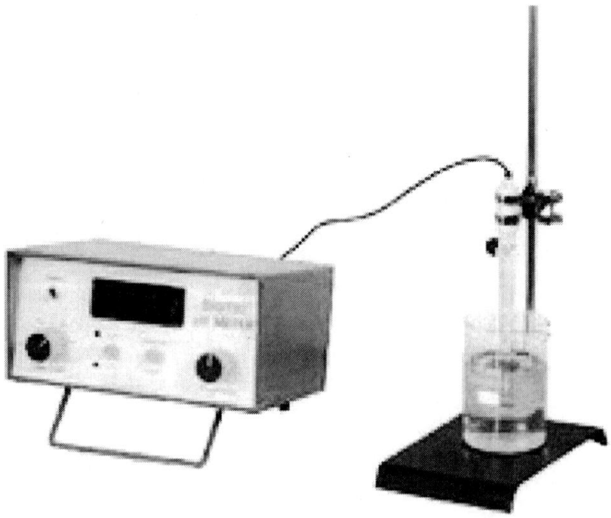

Electrodes of a pH meter

The pH meter has two electrodes

(a) Reference electrode (Calomel electrode)

(b) Glass electrode

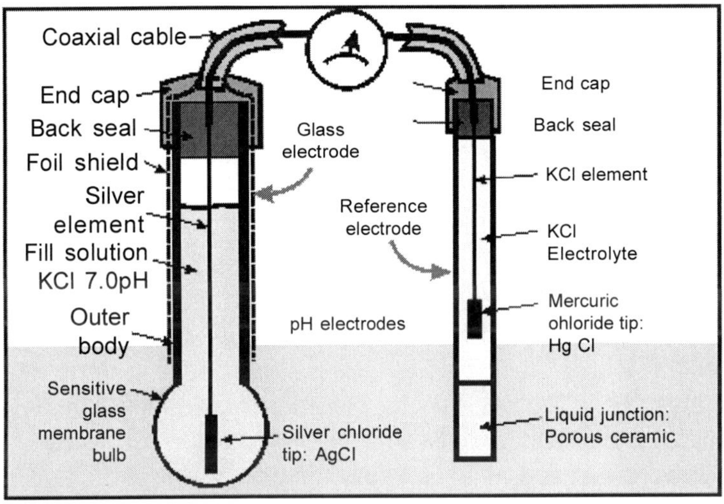

(a) Reference electrode

A reference electrode is an electrode that has the known half-cell potential constant and completely insensitive to the composition of solution under study. It provides standard voltage.

Characteristics of ideal reference electrode

- Reversible and obeys Nernst equation
- Exhibit a potential that is constant with time
- Return to its original potential after being subjected to small currents.

Reference electrode may be a calomel electrode containing $HgCl_2$ / Hg in the inner layer and the outer layer is filled with KCl solution in which chloride is used to maintain ionic strength.

Calomel electrode is an example of a half cell. It has a platinum wire immersed in slurry of solid $HgCl_2$ / Hg and aqueous saturated KCl. It has two layers. The inner tubes contain $HgCl_2$/Hg which is connected to a outer tube containing saturated KCl solution. The outer tube is connected to inner tube by small opening.

(b) Glass electrode

The outer electrode is called as glass electrode. It is also called as the indicator (or) working electrode. The response of this electrode depends upon the analyte concentration. The electromotive force (E.M.F.) of this glass electrode is determined by joining it with a reference electrode. The glass electrode contains a bulb like structure made up of soda lime glass which is sensitive to H^+.

When the glass electrode comes in contact with H^+ of test solution, it acquires an electrode potential which depends on the activity of H^+. Ag wire smeared with AgCl is immersed in ionisable electrolyte usually HCl.

Measurement of pH

When these two electrodes are dipped in solution, the saturated KCl comes out of the reference electrode through the small holes and forms an invisible ionic bridge between the electrodes through which current passes. The H^+ are absorbed by glass electrode and depending upon the activity of H^+ in the solution, an electrical potential will be developed. The potential difference between the reference electrode and glass electrode is measured as pH by suitable galvanometer.

Conductometry

Conductometry is a measurement of electrical conductivity of ionic solutions by applying electric current between two electrodes. Solutions of electrolytes conduct an electric current by the migration of positively charged species towards the cathode and negatively charged species towards the anode under the influence of an electric field. Solutions of strong acids, strong bases and most of the salts are good conductors of electric current. The conductometry estimation is based on Ohm's law.

$$C \alpha \frac{1}{R}$$

Ohm's law states that the current flowing through a conductor between two points is directly proportional to the potential difference across the two points. For the same type of material, the resistance is directly proportional to the length of the conductor and inversely proportional to the cross section. The resistance (R) is expressed in Ohm's and the conductance of the solution is the reciprocal of its resistance and is expressed as mhos

$$R \alpha \frac{L}{A}$$

Where,

R = Resistance

L = Distance between the electrodes

A = Cross sectional area of the conductor

$$R = \nu \times \frac{L}{A}$$

Where

ν = proportionality constant known as electrical resistivity
If L = 1 cm, A = 1 cm^2

Then R = r, Where r = specific resistivity

Electrical conductivity meter

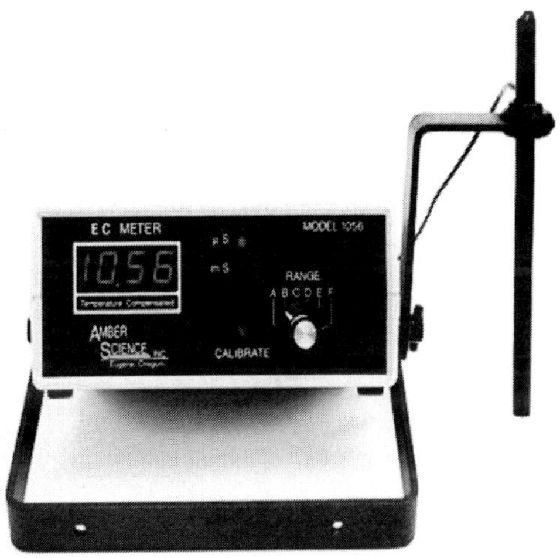

Specific resistance

It is the resistance of a conductor 1 cm in length and 1 cm^2 in area. Higher the salt content, higher the passage of current and lesser the resistance to the flow of current.

$$R = \alpha \frac{1}{Salt\ content}$$

The reciprocal of specific resistivity is called as specific conductivity.

Specific conductivity

It is defined as the conductivity of a solution enclosed in a cell whose electrodes are exactly 1cm and posses a surface area of 1 cm^2. It is not possible to make a conductivity bridge having electrodes 1 cm^2 in area and exactly 1 cm apart. Hence, the factor called cell constant is determined in the given cells.

Equivalent conductance

It is the conductance of a solution containing one gram equivalent weight of dissolved electrolyte between electrodes 1 cm apart.

$$\text{Equivalent conductance} = \frac{\text{Specific conductance}}{\text{Normality}} \times 1000$$

Chapter 12

Principles and Practices of Colorimetry and Spectrophotometry

Colorimetry is the quantitative analysis of a coloured constituent. It is determined by measuring the relative amount of absorption of light passing through a solution of a constituent.

When a monochromatic light is passed through a homogeneous medium, a part of the incident light is absorbed and part of the light is reflected and part could be transmitted. This can be mathematically expressed as,

$$I_O = I_a + I_t + I_r$$

Where,

I_O = Intensity of incident light

I_a = Intensity of light absorbed

I_t = Intensity of light transmitted

I_r = Intensity of reflected light

This relationship is used in colorimetry wherein the quantity of a coloured constituent is determined by measuring the relative amount of absorbed light by optical density (OD) (or) transmittance (T) with reference to the known concentration of the substance.

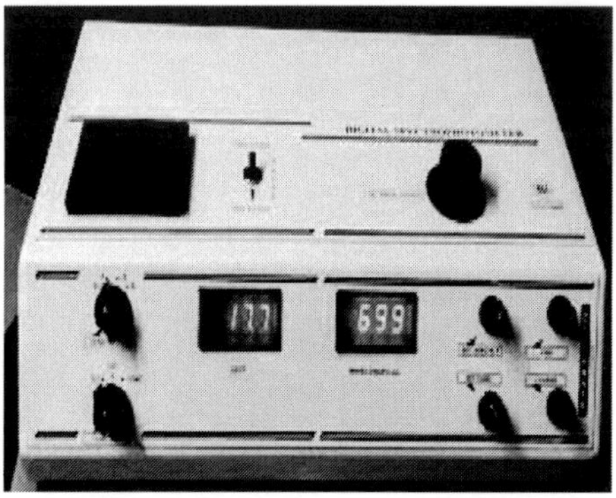

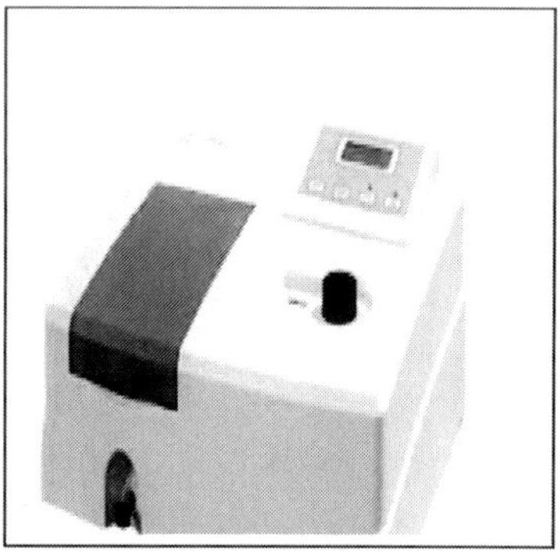

Basic principles of colorimetry

Two basic principles (Laws) are involved

a. Lambert's law

b. Beer's law

(a) Lambert's law

When a monochromatic light passes through an absorbing medium, its intensity decreases exponentially as the length of the medium increases.

$$I = I_0 . e^{-kt}$$

Where

I = Intensity of light absorbed

I_0 = Incident light

k – Absorption coefficient

t – Thickness (length) of the medium

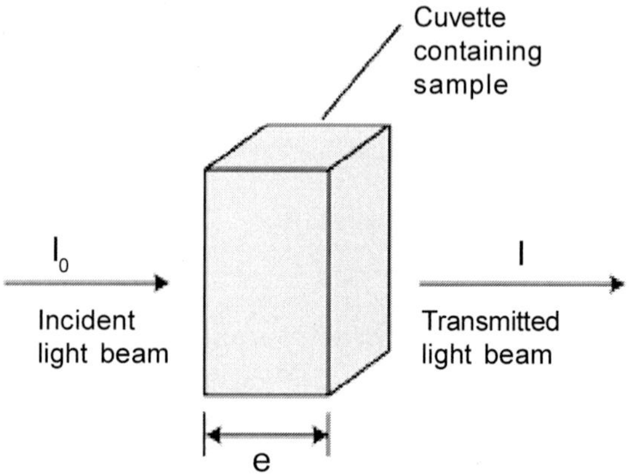

(b) Beer's Law

When a monochromatic light passes through an absorbing medium, its intensity decreases exponentially as the concentration of the absorbing medium increases.

$$I = I_0 . e^{-k/c}$$

Where,

I = Intensity of transmitted light

I_o = Incident light

k = constant

c = concentration of solution

(c) Beer's and Lambert's law

The Beer's and Lambert's law states that the concentration of a substance in solution is directly proportional to the absorbance (A) of the solution.

$$I_t = I_0 10^{-Ect}$$

$$\text{Log}_{10} \frac{I_0}{I} = Ect = abc$$

Where a = estimation coefficient

b = thickness (length) of the medium

c = concentration of the medium (solution)

Colorimeter

Components

a) A source of radiant energy

b) Filter for isolation of a band of radiant energy

c) An optical system for producing a parallel beam of filtered light

d) A detector

e) Read out meters

Components of Colorimeter

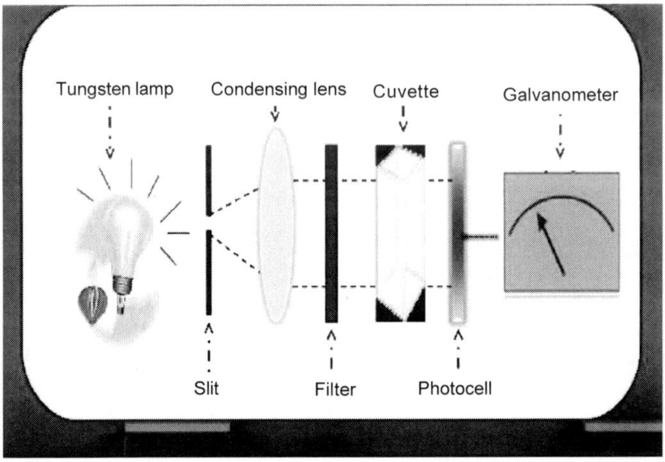

Measurement

In the colorimeter, the monochromatic light passing through a filter is passed through water / blank solution and the instrument is adjusted to 100% transmittance (or) zero optical density. Then the solution containing colour producing substance (chromogen) at various concentration is placed in the light path and the optical density/ transmittance is measured from the scale and a standard graph is prepared. Then the solution with unknown concentration is placed and the optical density / transmittance is read from the scale. By referring the standard graph, the actual concentration of unknown solution is determined.

Applications

- Used for determining minute quantities of substances.
- Commonly used to estimate available phosphorus in soil, P content of plant sample, chlorophyll estimation, protein content of any substances.

Spectrophotometry

Spectrophotometers are used to measure the intensity of specific spectral line of the light. The basic principles involved are Beer's and Lambert's law.

Principle

When a monochromatic light passes through a solution the intensity of light transmitted is inversely proportional to the concentration of the element / absorption of light is directly proportional to the concentration of the substance.

$$T \alpha \frac{1}{C}$$

$$A \alpha C$$

$$A \alpha \frac{1}{T}$$

Schematic diagram of Spectrophotometry

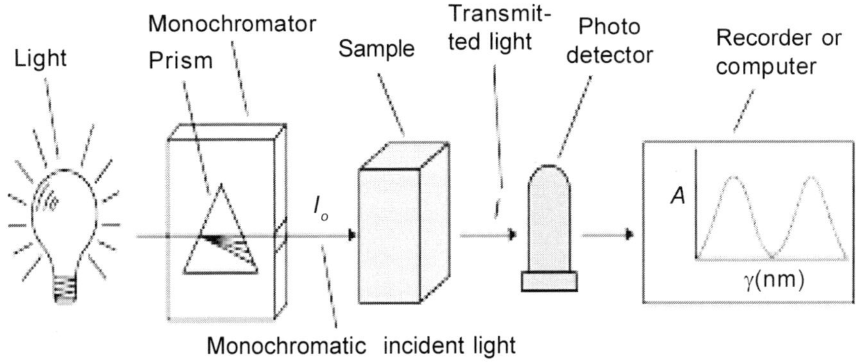

Types of spectrophotometers

There are 2 types of spectrophotometers

a. Infrared spectrophotometer(IR spectrophotometer)

b. Ultra-violet spectrophotometer (UV spectrophotometer)

In IR spectrophotometer, infrared source is used. Whereas, in UV spectrophotometer, both visible and UV radiation source is used.

(a) Infra red spectrophotometer

In this instrument, the source of radiant energy is Nernst glower. It consists of a mixture of Zirconium and Yttrium oxides in the shape of a tube which is electrically heated to 1500-2000°C. Because infrared rays are not transmitted by glass, a prism of salt (NaCl) is used as a monochromator. The radiations from Nernst glower are polychromatic and when passed through the salt prism, the wavelengths get separated. A slit is placed in the form of radiation emerging from the prism, so that, only radiant energy of desired wavelength passes through and falls on to the solution under test. The radiant energy transmitted by the solution is allowed to fall on a detector. Thermal detectors are used for measuring the intensity of transmitted infrared radiation.

(b) U.V. spectrophotometer

This type of spectrophotometer covers the range of 220-1000 nm, which includes ultraviolet, visible and near IR regions. The source of radiant energy is a tungsten lamp (for visible region) and a deuterium lamp (for UV region). A prism made up of silica is used as a monochromator. The intensity of the beam transmitted by the sample solution is measured by a photocell. A glass prism cannot be used because glass does not transmit ultraviolet light. A silica prism is suitable for both visible and ultraviolet radiations.

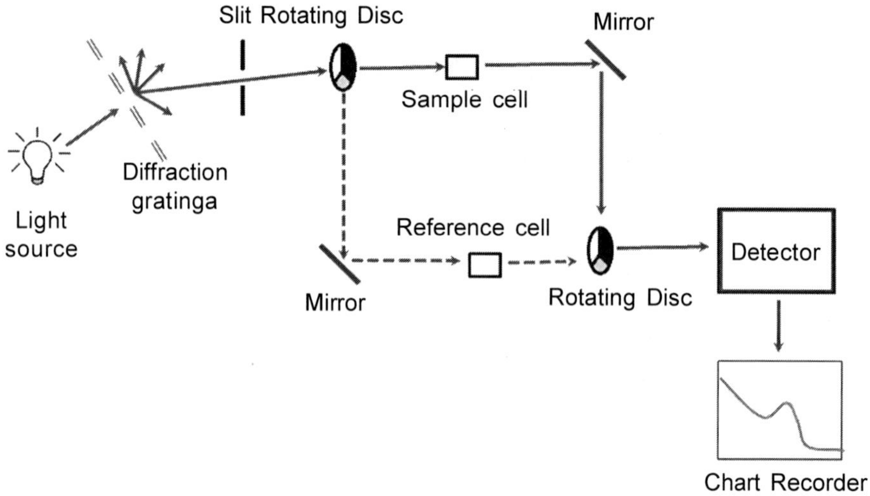

Components of spectrophotometer

Spectrophotometer consists of 2 instruments.

a) Spectrometer

b) Photometer

(a) Spectrometer – For producing light of any selected wavelength

(b) Photometer – For measuring the intensity of light

The instruments are arranged so that liquid in a cuvette can be placed between spectrometer beam and photometer. The amount of light passing through the tube is measured by photometer which delivers a voltage signal to a display device, normally a galvanometer.

The essential parts of spectrophotometer are

1. Source – An incandescent lamp with a tungsten filament is used as a source for visible region, near I.R and near U.V.

2. Monochromator – It transmits only narrow band of wavelength to pass through and is usually done by prisms.

   - Visible region – Glass prisms.
   - U.V, near I.R. and visible – Quartz prism

3. Sample container – Glass cells for visible region, quartz (or) special silica glass for UV region and rock salt cells for IR region.
4. A detector - Photoelectric detectors for visible, UV and thermoelectric detectors for IR region.
5. Amplifier
6. Readout system

Measurement by using spectrophotometer

- The intensity of light (Io) passing through a blank is measured. The blank is a solution without the solute that absorbs light. This measurement is necessary because the cell itself scatters some of the light.
- The intensity of light (I) passing through the sample solution is measured
- Experimental data is used to calculate two quantities such as
  - Transmittance (T)
  - Absorbance (A)

$$T = \frac{I}{I_o}$$

$$A = -\log_{10} T$$

- Transmittance – Fraction of light in the original beam that passes through
- The remainder of light, 1 – T, is the fraction of the light absorbed by the sample.

Advantage

- Less proceduce
- Rapid and accurate
- Less energy involved

Advantages of spectrophotometer

- Determines very low concentration (< 0.001 μg)
- Less procedure
- Less energy involved
- Rapid and accurate

Chapter 13

Principles and Practices of Absorption and Emission Spectroscopy

Absorption and Emission

Absorption techniques – It measures the absorption of abundance of light due to electrons going to a higher energy level.

Emission techniques - It measures the intensity of light that is emitted as electrons return to the lower energy levels.

Absorption spectroscopy

It is the method of determining the concentration of an element in a sample by measuring the absorption of radiation by the atomic vapour from the sample at a wave length that is specific and characteristic of the element under consideration. The basis in the absorption of energy by neutral atoms in ground state when they are in gaseous form.

Emission spectroscopy

When the sample is excited electrically to burn in an arc (or) thermally in a flame it produces (or) emits spectrum characteristic of its component metals (emission spectrum) which when passed through a dispersing system of a spectrograph, the intensity of individual lines spectrum can be measured.

(A) Flame photometry /Flame Emission Spectroscopy

It is the study of light (photon) energy emitted when a metal is introduced into the flame. Radiation in the visible and ultraviolet regions occur when the atoms or molecules are excited by the absorption of energy.

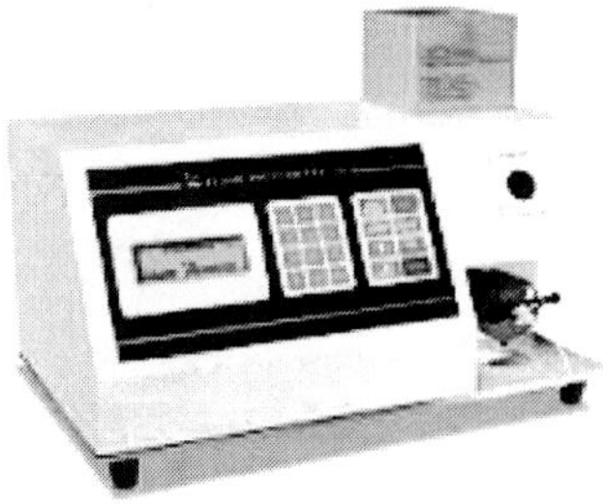
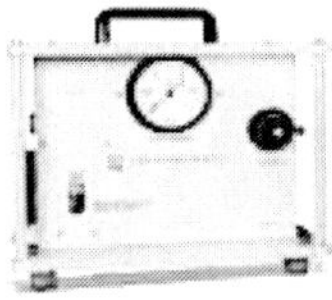
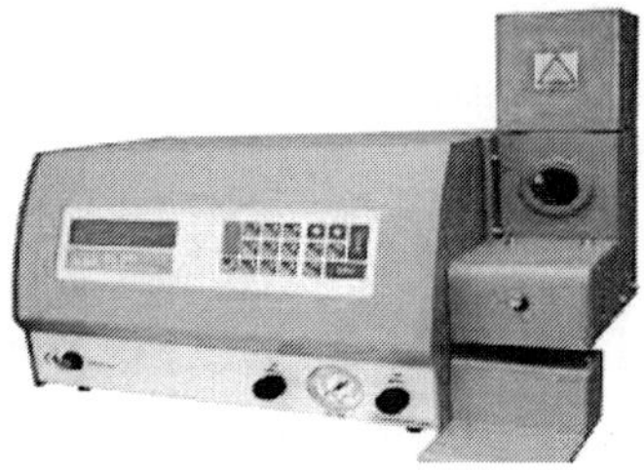

Principle

When an alkali metal is excited in a non luminous flame, electrons from the inner orbit jump towards the outer most orbit and after loosing the energy it return to the ground state, then emit radiations of characteristic wave length in the form of photons. The intensity of emission is directly proportional to the concentration of the element in the solution. Each element emits radiation at a specific wavelength.

Element emission wavelength (nm) and flame colour

Element	Emission wavelength (nm)	Flame colour
Na	589	Yellow
K	766	Lilac (Blue)
Ba	554	Lime green
Ca	622	Brick red
Li	670	Red

Components of a flame photometer

(a) Atomizer

This is a device to introduce liquid sample into the flame for conversion into vapour form. The passage of O_2 from the tip causes the solution to be drawn up to inner capillary tube where it disappeared into fine droplets. Approximately, 1-2 ml of the sample is consumed in 1 minute.

(b) Burner

The main requirement of burner is when supplied with fuel and air at constant pressure, it should produce a steady flame.

The flame produced

1. Transforms the sample to be analyzed from liquid state into gaseous state.
2. Decomposes molecular compounds of element into simpler molecules (or) atoms
3. Excites the atoms to light emission.

(c) Pressure regulators and flow meters for fuel gases

Pressure or flow rate of the gas is controlled by pressure regulator. The pressure gauge indicate the pressure and flow rate. A 10 lb gauge for the fuel and 25 lb gauge for O_2 air supply are generally satisfactory. A change in quantity of fuel or) air flowing into the burner varies the flame characteristics and the reproducibility of results is affected.

(d) Optical system

The optical system collects the light from steadiest part of the flame, converts it into monochromatic, and then focuses it into the surface of photosensitive detector.

(e) Photosensitive detector

Photocell (or) photomultiplier tube detection system converts the light energy, into electronic pulses and measured. Photocell detector is used when a wide band of radiant energy strike the detector. When the band width reaching the detector is less, phototubes can be used to amplify and detect the radiation.

Working principle of flame photometer

The liquid containing metallic salt solution is introduced into a flame, the following sequence of events occur.

1. Water (or) other solvent is vapourized, leaving a minute particle of dry salt
2. At high flame temperature, the dry salt is vapourized and the gaseous molecules are dissociated to give neutral atoms.

3. The vapours of neutral atoms are excited by thermal energy of flame.
4. The excited atoms are unstable and return back to their original position by spontaneous emission of light
5. Collection and detection of emitted light energy and converts into electronic pulses.

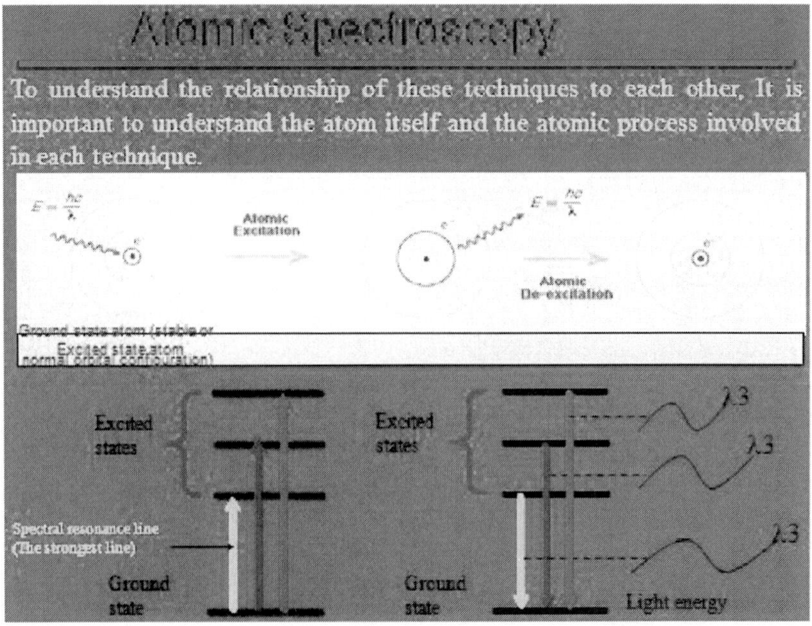

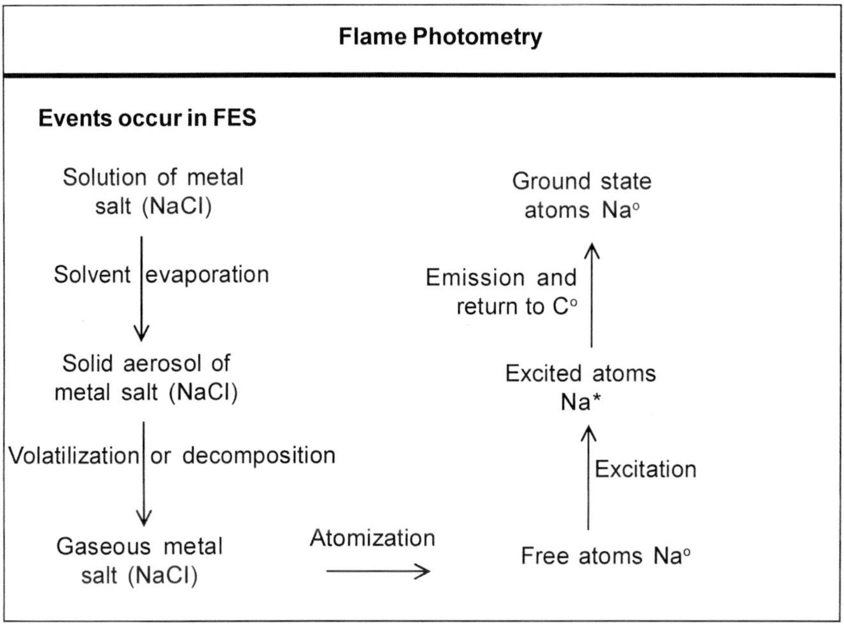

Disadvantage of flame photometer

- Spectral interferences – A rise from the close proximity of other emission lines (or) bands which can be minimized by increasing the resolution of instrumentation.
- **Example** : Changing from filter photometer to gravity spectrophotometer.
- Chemical interference by other elements – The presence of species in the flame other than those of the analyte may alter the emitted intensities of analyte through chemical interferences.

  Example : SO_4^{2-}, NO_3^{-}, PO_4^{3-}

Addition of chelating agents is the better way of eliminating such effects because the chelating agents protect the metal from the interfering ion.

- Self absorption- It is a phenomenon where the emitted radiation is reabsorbed as it passes outwards from the central region of the flame.
- Fluctuation in flame temperature – Intensity of emission is very sensitive to changes in flame temperature.

Merits of flame photometer

Flame photometer are generally employed for estimating alkali and alkaline earth metals such as Na, K, Ca, Li, Rb, Cs, Ba.

(B) Atomic Absorption Spectrophotometer (AAS)

It is a method of determination of an element in a sample by measuring the absorption of radiation by the atomic vapour produced from the sample at a wavelength that is specific and characteristic of the element under consideration. The basis is the absorption of energy by neutral atoms in ground state when they are in gaseous form. Absorption is directly proportional to the concentration.

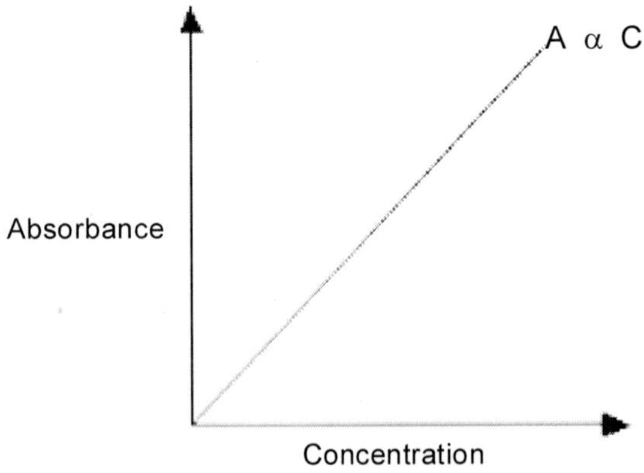

Atomic Absorption Spectrophotometer (AAS) is commoly used to estimate micronutrients like Fe, Mn, Zn, Cu, Mo etc.

Atomic Absorption Spectrophotometer (AAS)

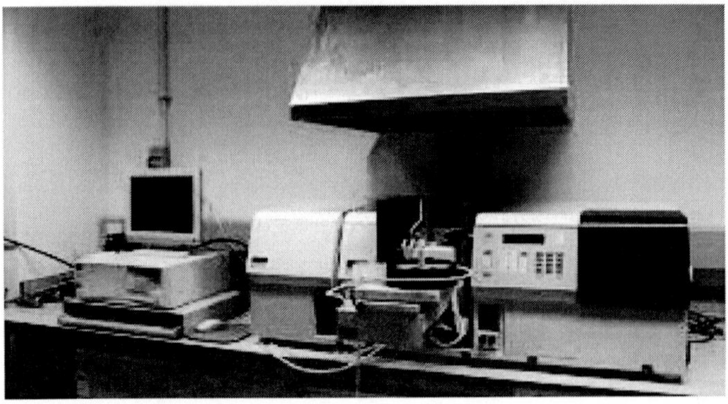

Principle

When light from a suitable source is directed through the atomic cloud of the sample, the detector measures the quantity of light absorbed by measuring the intensity of radiation before and after it is passed through the sample. The atoms of the sample is converted into gaseous form and absorbs energy in proportion to the density of atoms. The change in intensity of light gives the amount of energy absorbed by the atoms.

Components of AAS

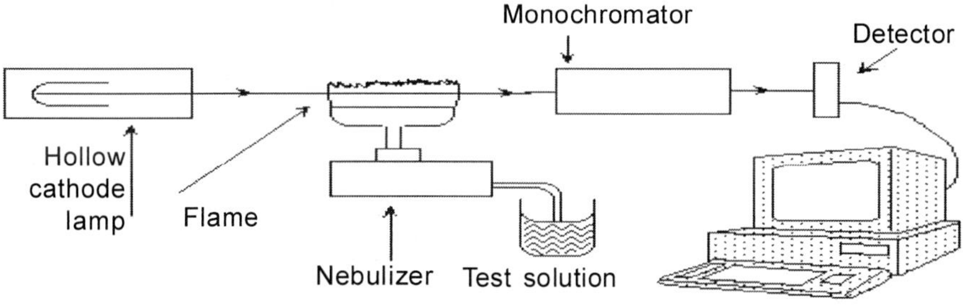

1. Radiation source (Hollow cathode lamp)

The radiation source is a hollow cathode lamp which generates the radiation and this is absorbed by dissociated atoms. The line should be sufficiently spectral purity and intensity to achieve a linear calibration graph with low noise level. The hollow cathode lamp is filled with a rare gas generally Ar or Ne at low pressure, has its cathode made of (or) lined with other element (or) elements to be estimated. The hollow cathode lamps emit only the spectrum of the cathode element together with that of the filled gas. The anode is a straight metal wire. The front face of the lamp is made up of quartz.

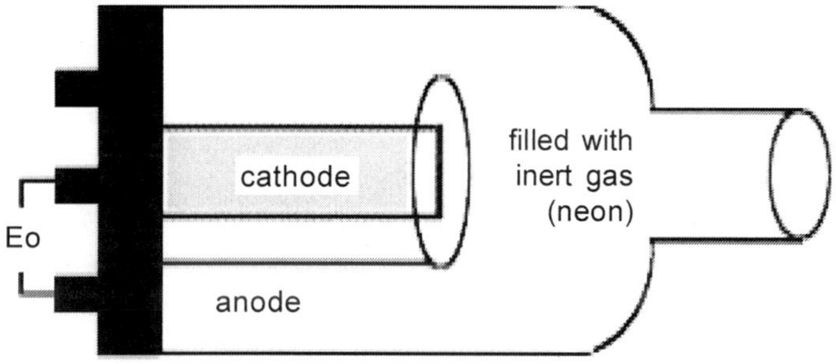

The cathode is covered with the element of interest

2. Flame atomization system

The important parts of the flame atomization system are

(a) Nebulizer

The main functions of the nebulizers are

- To draw up solution
- Regulate uptake rate

- Convert solution into aerosol
- Provide main pathway for the oxidant gas.

(b) Burner and flame

The only purpose of a burner and flame is to get the element to be estimated into atomic state. Burners used for AAS are all the premix, laminar flow type. The sample aerosol is aspirated and mixed with the gases before combustion. During combustion, the element is reduced to the atomic state and it can absorb radiation. Flames in uses are normally produced by two types of gas mixtures. Air – acetylene and nitrous oxide – acetylene. Air – acetylene is the cooler flame (2100 – 2400°C) and this is used for those elements that do not form refractory compounds and have relatively low ionization potentials. Nitrous oxide – acetylene is a hotter flame (2600 to 2800°C) and must be used for elements forming refractory compounds (Eg. SiO_2, Al_2O_3, TiO_2, Cr_2O_3).

3. Monochromator

To obtain a linear relationship between absorbance and concentration, it is essential to isolate the line to be measured from all other lines.

4. Detector

Wavelength for common elements

Elements	Wave length of absorption
Zn	213.9
Fe	248.3
Mn	279.5
Cu	324.8
Cd	223.8
Ni	232.0
Cr	357.9
Pb	288.3

Disadvantages of AAS

- Individual source lamps are required for each element
- Sample must be in solution (or) volatile.

Chapter 14

Principles and Practices of Chromatography

Chromatography is the set of laboratory techniques used for the separation of molecular mixtures by developing chromatograms. Chromatogram is a collection of different bands on the chromatographic column. The mixture is dissolved in a fluid called the "mobile phase", which carries with it another material called the "stationary phase". The various constituents of the mixture travel at different speeds, causing them to separate. Chroma (colour) and graph in (to write) contribute to the word **chromatography**, as coined by Mikhail Tswett (1903). Solute moves only when it is in stationary phase. In chromatography, the mobile phase flowing into the column is called **eluent**, the solution emerging from the column is **elute,** and the process by which solutes moves and separate is called **elution**.

This method employs the differences in absorbability of components of mixtures and the differences in the mobility rate. The molecules of a substance which interact strongly with the fixed phase will move slowly through the column whereas substances which do not interact strongly are carried through more rapidly. It is used to separate different substances having similar chemical properties.

Terms in Chromatography

- **Analyte** is the substance to be separated during chromatography.
- **Bonded phase** is a stationary phase that is bonded to the support particles or to the inside wall of the column tubing.
- **Chromatogram** is the visual output of the chromatograph. In the case of an optimal separation, different peaks or patterns on the chromatogram correspond to different components of the separated mixture.

- **Chromatograph** is the equipment that enables a sophisticated separation e.g. gas chromatographic or liquid chromatographic separation.
- **Chromatography** is a physical method of separation in which the components to be separated are distributed between two phases, one of which is stationary (stationary phase) while the other (the mobile phase) moves in a definite direction.
- **Eluate** is the mobile phase leaving the column.
- **Eluent** is the solvent that carries the analyte.
- **Solute** refers to the sample components in partition chromatography.
- **Solvent** refers to any substance capable of solubilizing other substance
- **Stationary phase** is the substance which is fixed in place for the chromatography procedure. Eg. S layer in thin layer chromatography
- **Mobile phase** serves to carry the sample molecules through the chromatographic column.
- **Retention time** is the time taken for a particular compound to travel through the column to the detector. This time is measured from the time at which the sample is injected to the point at which the display shows a maximum peak height for that compound.

Branches of chromatography

(i). Based on the phases of chromatography – As mobile and stationary phase

Mobile	Stationary	Type of Chromatograhy
Gas	Liquid	Gas – Liquid Chromatography
Gas	Solid	Gas – Solid Chromatography
Liquid	Liquid	Liquid – Liquid Chromatography
Liquid	Solid	Liquid - Solid Chromatography

The first two types (1 and 2) are generally referred as **gas phase chromatography or simply gas chromatography** and the last two as liquid-phase chromatography.

(ii). Based on mechanism of retention

1. **Adsorption chromatography:** It is based on selective adsorption of separate components of a mixture. A insoluble solid in the solvent is used as stationary phase.

2. **Partition chromatography:** The stationary phase is supported by a porous substance (carrier) and the other phase is a (solvent) liquid which is immiscible with the first liquid. Distribution of components in a mixture occurs due to differences in solubility.

3. **Ion exchange chromatography:** It is mainly based on the ion exchange phenomena. The mobile phase may be a liquid or a gas which can be forced through the fixed phase by pressure

(iii). Based on physical configuration

1. **Column chromatography:** The stationary phase is a solid (column packed with adsorbents such as alumina or silica gel) and the mobile phase is a liquid. The basis for separation is selective adsorption of the components present in the liquid phase on solid. Eg. Gas chromatography

2. **Planar chromatography:** The stationary phase is a thin two-dimensional sheet and the mobile phase is a liquid. Eg. Paper chromatography

(iv). Based on sample development

1. **Frontal chromatography:** The sample is fed to the column continuously and it emerges as fronts

2. **Displacement chromatography:** It is a chromatography technique in which a sample is placed onto the head of the column and is then displaced by a solute that is more strongly sorbed than the components of original mixture.

3. **Elution chromatography :** The separation of sample is obtained by different fractions of time spent by the components of sample in a mobile phase. It gives good separation of compounds and leaves the column in its original condition.

Common chromatographic methods

a. Paper chromatography

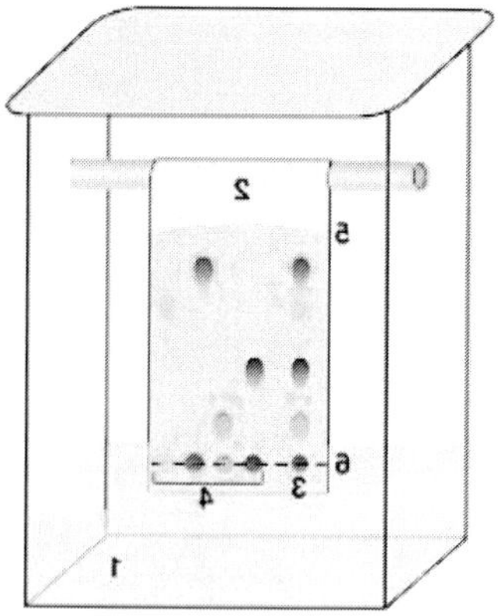

Paper chromatography is a technique that involves placing a small dot or line of sample solution onto a strip of chromatography paper. The paper is placed in a jar containing a shallow layer of solvent and sealed. As the solvent rises through the paper by capillary action, it meets the sample mixture which starts to travel up the paper with solvent. This paper is made of cellulose, a polar substance, and the compounds within the mixture travel farther if they are non-polar.

When the solvent reaches the top-edge of the paper (solvent front), the paper is removed and dried in an oven. The separated spots, if colourless may be rendered visible by treatment with an appropriate reagent. Eg. separation of amino acids

Retention Factor (RF): The retention factor (R_f) may be defined as the ratio of the distance traveled by the substance to the distance traveled by the solvent.

$$Rf = \frac{\text{Distance travelled by the component}}{\text{Distance travelled by the solvent}}$$

Applications- Suitable for the rapid analysis of amino acids

(B) Thin layer chromatography (TLC)

This method is used to identify the compounds. Confirmation by TLC is based on comparison of migration distances of an analyte with authentic standards run of the same layer.

Principle

A drop of unknown sample is placed on a thin glass plate which is uniformly coated with a layer of absorbing material like silica gel or alumina gel or cellulose and the plate is immersed in a mobile phase. This results in the upward movement of mobile phase and the sample separates by its differential absorptive power. The materials which are having low absorptive power move fast and come to the top and others remain at the bottom. The separated materials are then analysed colorimetrically or by spraying chemicals on them or by radioactive methods.

Procedure

- **Preparation of TLC plates:** By means of a plate spreader, the slurry of the stationary phase in water is applied as a thin coat on a glass plate. The layer is of the order of 0.25 mm thickness. A binding agent such as calcium sulphate is incorporated in the slurry when the stationary phase is used for absorption chromatography. This is to facilitate the adhesion of the absorbent to the plate. The coated plate is air dried and is activated in the oven at 110°C for 45 minutes.
- **Sample application:** The sample is applied to the plate by means of micropipette or syringe at one edge of the plate.
- **Plate development:** The plate is dipped to a depth of 1.5 cm of developing solvent, for an hour in a closed environment. After the solvent has reached the top edge of the plate, it is removed and dried.
- **Component detection:** Spraying of plates with specific colour reagents will stain up certain compounds. If the compounds are radioactive, the plates may be subjected to autoradiography which will detect the spots as dark areas in X-ray film. Irradiation of the plate with ultra violet light permit location of spots of compounds that exhibit fluorescence.

Applications

- Ideal for routine – analysis of mixture composition.
- Very small quantity (10^{-9} g) is required
- To find out the best eluting agent for column chromatography.
- By visual comparison of sample and standard spot sizes / intensities
- More accurate quantification can be carried out by inside scanning of spots with a spectro densitometer
- Individual ions can be identified.

Merits

- Simple and rapid
- Low cost
- Sensitivity ranges from 5-500 ug

(C) High Performance Thin Layer Chromatography(HPTLC)

It is an enhanced form of TLC and is used for separations and insitu quantitative analysis. HPTLC is carried out on 10x10 cm or 5x5 cm layers of silica gel with a smaller particle size and a narrower particle size distribution than in conventional TLC plates and thereby gives improved resolution and sensitivity of detection. Volumes not larger than 1 µl must be spotted to realize best results. For manual application, spotting is usually done with a Pt-Fe tipped nano pipette or equivalent or this type of pipette is used with an automatic spotting device that control both the pressure of the pipette tip on the layer and the duration of contact. Solvent development is carried out in the miniature glass rectangular chamber. High resolution is achieved rapidly with short development distances.

(D) Gas Chromatography (GC) or Gas Liquid Chromatography (GLC)

Principle

It is widely used for the separation of volatile compounds. Gas chromatography (GC), also sometimes known as Gas-Liquid chromatography, (GLC), is a separation technique in which the mobile phase is a gas.

Basic Components

1. **Carrier gas assembly:** The chemically pure inert gases viz., helium, nitrogen, hydrogen and argon are used to minimize background signals. Flow rate and pressure level desired usually are 5 to 50 ml / min and 10 to 50 psi, respectively.
2. **Sample injection port:** To enable the volatilization of the sample quickly, the sample is injected through a self sealing rubber septum which is maintained at a specified temperature. The injection is performed using micro syringe of capacity ranging from 0.1 to 5 µl.

3. **Columns:** Long tubes of metals like Cu, stainless steel, Al or glass are used as columns.
4. **Thermal compartment:** The temperature of the column will be maintained at a temperature, slightly higher than the point of evaporation of the sample substance.
5. **Detector system:** Once the sample is vaporized, it passes through detectors like Flame Ionization Detector (FID) or Thermal Conductivity Detector (TCD) which produces electric impulses which are amplified and recorded.
6. **Thermal conductivity detector (TCD)** – It consists of an electrically heated wire which assumes a steady temperature and resistance when the pure gas flows over it. As the separated components reach the wire, the change in resistance is measured.
7. **Flame ionization detector (FID)** – It is sensitive over TCD. It is sensitive, fairly stable and responsive to all organic compounds. The ions produced by organic compounds results in an ion current which is measured.
8. **Electron capture detector (ECD)** – Certain molecules absorb free atoms emitted by radio active sources. When an electron capturing solute enters the ECD cell, the standing current decreases because of the consumption of free electrons by electron capturing process. The decrease in standing current is sensed by the detector. Used in determining halogens, peroxides, quinones and metal organic compounds.
9. **Monitor:** The data through electric impulses can be recorded using a mobile pen in the graph.

The area of peak can be measured by using standards and the sample contents can be quantified.

Working principle

Gas chromatography is always carried out in a column, which is a packed column or capillary column. The mixture to be separated is vapourised and sent through the column by flowing inert gases such as hydrogen or helium called carrier gas. This unit is individually heated to facilitate vaporization of the sample. The gaseous mixture is the mobile phase. As the vaporized sample is swept into the column by the carrier gas its components separate into individual bands due to selective phase distribution between two phases, gets separated and pass into the detector.

Applications

- Applicable for qualitative and quantitative identification of components in a mixture
- Study of atmospheric pollutants and separation of aromatic amines
- Used for purification of a compound as an alternative to distillation
- Sensitive and simple and the gases permit the use of very long columns, thereby improving the efficiency of separation.
- The gases do not have interaction with the solute.
- Relatively volatile substances can easily be analysed.

E. High Performance Liquid Chromatography (HPLC)

High performance liquid chromatography is basically a highly improved form of column chromatography. Instead of a solvent being allowed to drip through a column under gravity, it is forced through under high pressures of up to 400 atmospheres. The liquid chromatography using high efficiency columns at high pressure is known as HPLC. The instrument is expensive as it is operated under very high pressure.

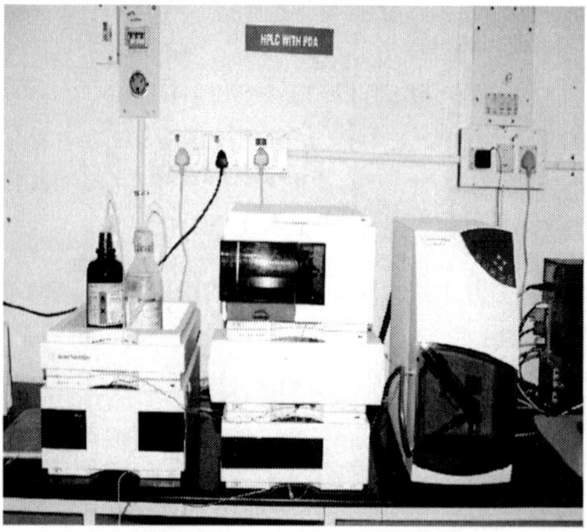

Advantages of HPLC over Gas Chromatography

- The sample constituents need not be volatile or thermally stable at higher temperatures.
- The mobile phase (liquid) interacts with the sample constituents and therefore has a direct effect on the distribution coefficients; whereas in gas chromatography, the solute distribution is largely independent of the carrier gas.

Components of HPLC

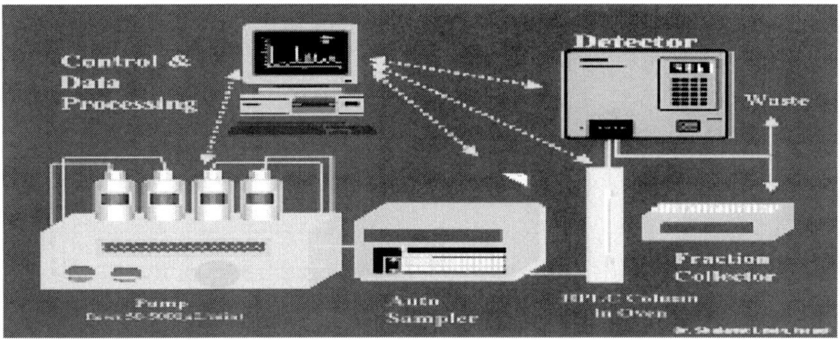

Stationary and mobile phase

The mobile phase which is a liquid is pumped at high pressure into a controlled temperature oven, to bring it to operating temperature and to remove impurities. As in gas chromatography the sample is added to the mobile phase just prior to the column. The column effluent is passed through the detector and then to waste.

- **Stationary phase:** Siloxane is used as stationary phase. It is prepared by heating silica particles in dilute acid for a day or two to generate reactive silonal group.
- The liquid **mobile phase** should have the following properties
- Low viscosity to facilitate easy flow
- High purity to avoid contamination of the sample
- High chemical stability to avoid side reactions with solutes or stationary phase.
- Low volatility to avoid the formation of bubbles in the column / detector
- Immiscibility to avoid the dissolution of the stationary liquid phase
- Compatibility with the different types of detectors.

Some of the examples for mobile phase are cyclohexane, n-hexane, carbontetra chloride, toluene, chloroform, ethanol, ether, methanol and water.

Pump

Most important and most expensive part of HPLC. Fluid flow essential for HPLC separation is accomplished with a high pressure pump. It should provide constant flow at different rates with minimal pulsations at low and high pressures. Slower the solvent flow rate better is the separation. A typical flow rate is 0.5-2.0 ml/min

HPLC Output

- **Eluent delivery system**: It consists of a degassing chamber and a pumping unit to produce a pressure of 10,000 psi at a pulse rate.
- **Sample inlet injection system**: A special device called 'stop flow injection' is generally used to avoid 'blow back' of the samples.
- **Columns:** The columns will be of 10 to 50 cm length, 2 to 10 mm inner diameter and made up of chemically inert and pressure endurable materials like stainless steel. Columns are housed in circulating air or water, to maintain a desirable temperature range of 30 to 1500° C.

Separation mechanisms: The important separation mechanisms in HPLC are

- Partition (separation by the property of polarity)
- Adsorption (by adsorption force in the case of non – polar compounds)
- Ion exchange (by using ion exchange materials)
- Size exclusion (by size exclusion techniques)

Detectors: Mostly the detectors used in HPLC function based on the optical properties of solutes, like refraction of light (refractive index detector) absorption of light (UV absorption detector), fluorescence (fluorescence detector) etc.

Recorder: Records the output with a variety of automatic peak integration

Working principle

The components to be separated are first dissolved in a liquid solvent and then forced to flow through chromatographic column under high pressure. The mixture is resolved in this column into its components and eluted at differential rate depending upon the extent of interaction with the stationary phase. Depending upon the component elution the detector provides electrical out put signals, which will be recorded in the recorder as peaks. Useful to determine amino acids, proteins, CHO, phenols, pesticides, growth regulators,antibiotics, metal organic and inorganic substances.

Merits

- Extremely efficient in separation.
- Few micro liters / microgram of analyte is required
- Wide variety of material can be analyzed
- Suitable for thermally labile compounds
- Evaluation of isomers distribution

Chapter 15

Radiation Chemistry – Radioactivity

Radiation Chemistry is a branch of nuclear chemistry that deals with the study of chemical effects of radiation on matter.

Radio activity is the process by which an atomic nucleus of an unstable atom loses energy by emitting ionizing radiations (a, b, g radiations). It may be of

i. **Natural Radioactivity** is due to spontaneous disintegration of atoms giving out radiations. Eg. Thorium, Uranium

ii. **Artificial Radioactivity** is due to bombardment of non radioactive elements with á particle. It is called as induced radioactivity. Eg. ^{65}Zn, ^{32}P

Atom

It is the fundamental building block of chemical elements. An atom contains a dense, positively charged inner core called **nucleus** and outer domain in which **electrons** are in motion around the nucleus. The nucleus consists of protons and neutrons and is collectively called **nucleons**. The three most important subatomic particles are protons, neutrons and electrons.

The weight of nuclear particles are expressed in **atomic mass unit(amu)**. One amu is equivalent to 1/12th of the mass of the carbon atom and the value is $1.66x10^{-27}$ kg. In terms of the atomic mass unit, the mass of electron is equivalent to $5.49 x10^{-4}$ amu, the mass of proton and neutron is 1.0073 and1.0087 amu respectively.

Atomic particles

Proton: A nuclear particle with an atomic weight of approximately one amu carrying one elementary unit of positive charge.

Electron*:* A small particle with an atomic weight of approximately1/1800 that of a proton and carrying one elementary unit of negative charge.

Neutron: A particle with no charge and mass close to that of a proton. A free neutron is unstable.

Structure of atom

Atom derived from the Greek word 'atomos' means, it cannot be further subdivided. This word was derived some 2000 years ago. It was Democritus who gave the name atom. According to him all matters consist of tiny indestructible particles.

Atomic theory of John Dalton (1808)

- All matters consist of atoms
- Atoms are indivisible
- All atoms of a single element are similar in every respect and behave alike.
- Atoms can neither be created nor destroyed.

Atomic number (Z)

Atomic number of an element is equal to the number of protons present in the nucleus of the atom. It is equal to the number of electrons present in the extra nuclear path.

Mass number (A)

The total number of protons and neutrons in the nucleus of an atom is called as the Mass number.

Atomic Number (Z) = Number of protons (or) number of electrons

Mass Number (A) = Number of protons + Number of neutrons

Isotopes

Atoms of an element which have the same number of protons but different number of neutrons are called isotopes. Alternatively, it can be defined as the atoms of an element which have the same atomic number but different mass numbers. As isotopes have the same number of protons and electrons and so has same chemical properties. While denoting the isotope of an element, the element is written with atomic mass at the head and atomic number at the bottom.

Eg. $^{1}H_{1}$, $^{2}H_{1}$ $^{3}H_{1;}$ $^{14}C_{6}$ or $^{12}C_{6}$

More than 280 stable isotopes and more than 200 radio active isotopes have been identified.

Types of isotopes

i. Radioisotopes

The isotopes having unstable nuclei undergo spontaneous disintegration and give off atomic particles as a stream of radiation. Eg. ^{32}P,^{65}Zn. The main radiations are alpha (α), beta (β)and gamma (γ). The disintegration or decay of unstable atoms accompanied by emission of radiation is called Radioactivity. This was first discovered by Marie Curie. Nuclides possessing radioactivity are called as radio isotopes. The stability / radioactivity of isotopes are due to

1. **Odd-Even rule:** Neutrons and protons containing even number are highly stable. Odd-odd combinations are least stable.
2. **Magic no.:** Any nuclei having 2 no. of N and P are found to be highly stable. 2,8,20,28,50,82,126. These are called magic numbers. Whenever both the neutron and proton have magic number, then the nucleus is extremely stable. Eg. $^{16}O_8$
3. **N / P ratio :** There is optimum ratio of N and P for a nucleus to be stable. It is 1:1 in lower nuclei and 1.5:1 in higher nuclei.

ii. Stable isotopes

They are heavy isotopes, ie. atoms heavier than the normal nuclei. They are not radioactive. Common stable isotopes are ^{15}N, ^{18}O etc., Many elements have more than one stable isotope. Eg. ^{16}O,^{17}O, ^{18}O

Measurement of radioactive and stable isotopes

Radioactive isotopes are measured in terms of specific activity. **Specific activity** is the amount of radioactivity per unit weight or volume of the total element present.

Stable isotopes are measured by mass differences. It is expressed in terms of percentage atoms over natural abundance. For eg, natural environment has an ^{15}N abundance of 0.37% then the amount of ^{15}N in sample is expressed as % ^{15}N atoms over the natural abundance atoms ^{15}N

Isobars

Atoms which have the **same mass number** but **different atomic numbers** are called isobars. Eg. $^{40}Ar_{18}$, $^{40}K_{19}$ and $^{40}Ca_{20}$

Isotones

Atoms which have **different atomic numbers** and different atomic masses but the **same number of neutrons** and called isotones. Eg. $^{14}C_{6}$, $^{15}N_{7}$ and $^{16}O_{8}$

Characteristics of radiation

Alpha (α) rays

Alpha particles are helium nuclei carrying 2 positive charges.

Eg. Alpha emitters - Ru, Pu, Po, U

- It ionizes atoms in its path and as the particles are doubly charged, the ionization potential is high. Hence it is not used in biological research.
- The penetration power is very less as they dissipate energy along the path
- Easy to shield them, as even a few centimeters of air, a sheet of paper or the dead skin on one's fingers can stop them.
- Due to alpha emission, the atomic weight is reduced by 4 and the atomic number by 2.

  $^{210}Po_{24} \rightarrow {}^{206}Po_{24} + {}^{4}He_{2}$

Beta(β) rays : are high speed electrons emitted from the nuclei of an unstable atom.

Eg. ^{32}P, ^{14}C, ^{35}S, ^{28}Al and are commonly used in agricultural research

- It may be either negative (β^-) or positive and hence called as positrons.
- Like alpha particle, β particle causes ionization of matter. As the charge of β particle is only half of an α particle, the ionization is less than α particle.
- The mass of β particle is only 1/ 7000 of the mass of á particle and hence has greater penetrating power.
- During the interaction with matter, β particles are deflected backwards as much as 180° and is called back scattering

Gamma(γ) rays

Gamma rays are identical to X rays but gamma rays arise from the atomic nucleus. Gamma rays are of short wavelength and are characterized by high penetrating power enabling them to pass through several centimeters of lead. Gamma emitters are ^{59}Fe, ^{65}Zn, ^{60}Co, ^{54}Mn etc., and are commonly used in agricultural research

Comparison of properties of α, β and γ rays

Property	α rays	β rays	γ rays
Nature	Helium nuclei	Fast electrons	Electromagnetic radiation
Velocity	1/10th of the velocity of light	Velocity of light	Velocity of light
Penetrating power	low	moderate	High
Stopped by	Paper or 0.01mm thick aluminum sheet	1cm aluminum shoot	Several cm thick lead
Charge	2	-1	0
Atomic weight	4	1/1840	0

Energy of radiation

An important property of radiation is energy of radiation, which is expressed in terms of millions of electron volts (Mev). One Mev is equivalent to the kinetic energy acquired by an electron being accelerated through a potential difference of 1 million volts. Greater the energy of radiation, higher will be the penetrating power. Knowledge of the energy of radiation is required to decide the type of shielding required and to choose the radio assay method. In a nuclear reactor, the radio activity is produced by 2 methods.

1. **Neutron bombardment:** Here energy is produced and the vessel with stands the large amount of heat produced.
2. **Fission:** Nuclei of ^{235}U, ^{239}U etc. are divided into 2 smaller nuclei of roughly unequal size following the capture of a neutron.

$$^{235}U_{92} + ^{1}n_{0} \rightarrow ^{97}Zr_{40} + ^{137}Te_{52} + 2n + 176 \text{ Mev}$$

Units of Radioactivity

Quantity	Old Unit	SI unit	Equivalence
Radioactivity (measurement of the total radioactivity emitted by the source)	Curie((Ci)	Becquerel (Bq) (1dps)	$1Ci = 3.7x10^{10}$ Bq
Exposure	Roentgen(R) ($2.58x10^{-4}$ C/kg)	Coulomb /kg (C/kg)	$1R = 2.58x10^{-4}$ C/kg
Absorbed dose (measure of the amount of energy absorbed by the material subjected to radiation)	Rad (100 erg/gm)	Gray (Gy) (1J/kg)	1 Gy =100 Rad
Dose Equivalent (measure of the biological effect of the absorbed radiation on tissues)	rem	Sievert (SV)	1 Sv= 100 rem

As per the International Commission of Radiological Protection (ICRP) the maximum permissible radiation dose to which radiation workers can be exposed is **20 mSv/year**. For non radiation workers it is **2Sv/year**.

Radioactive decay

The radioactive decay may be caused by many factors

i. Negatron emission

When the neutrons are more than protons negatron emission takes place.

$N \rightarrow P^{+} + \beta + \gamma$ (antineutron)
(Negatron)

As a result, atomic number (Z) increases by 1. The neutron number decreases by 1. Mass number (A) remains the same.

$^{32}P_{17}\ ^{32}S_{16} + \beta$

$A_z X\ A_{z+1Y} + 1_b$

ii. Positron

When P > N. The excess P is to be shed off

$P \rightarrow n + \beta + +$ y (neutrino)
(positron)

Net result Z - decreases, N = increases by 1, A remains the same.

ii. Electron capture

Takes place when P > N Net result is Z decreases. N increases and A remains the same. X ray emitted consequent to rearrangement of particle electron. If the electron is from K shell it is called as K capture. The excess energy is shed as X rays.

iii. γ emission

Follow up of P or N or Electron capture. When one electron falls from the nearest outer orbit to the nucleus to attain stability an extra energy is released which is called γ-ray (this is electromagnetic in nature).

iv. α emission

Emitted by the radioactive isotopes of heavy elements having an atomic number > 83. By a emission the atomic number declines by 2 and the mass number declines by four units.

$$^{238}U_{92} \rightarrow {}^{234}U_{90} + {}_{4}He_{2}$$

Rate of disintegration and decay constant

Let N be the number of atoms at any time t and let d N be the number of atoms that disintegrate in a small interval of time dt.-

Negative sign indicates that the number of radioactive atoms decreases with time -

λ is the disintegration constant or decay constant

Log= - λ t (On integration)

Decay Constant

The radioactive decay is also represented by radioactive half life which indicates the time interval for half of the atoms of radioactive elements to decay or change to another form.

Half-life ($T_{1/2}$)

It is defined as the time taken by the radioactive nuclei to get reduced to one half of original activity. When the energy is small the half life is long.

Eg. ^{14}C-5670 years, ^{32}P-14.3 days

The half-life ($T_{1/2}$) and the disintegration constant (λ) are connected by the following relationship T 1/2 = log 2/ decay constant.

Half-life period of radio isotopes

Radioisotope	Half life
^{32}P	14.3 days
^{65}Zn	245 days
^{35}S	86.7 days
^{3}H	12.26 years
^{14}C	5720 years
^{137}Cs	30 years

Henri Becquerel : Discoverer of radioactivity

Marie Curie & Pierre Curie: Discoverers of radium and polonium.

Chapter 16

Detection and Measurement of Radioactivity – Radiological Safety

Radiation emitted from the radioactive isotopes can be detected and quantified by using several equipments and the details are furnished below:

A. Radiation Detection Devices

1. Electroscope

The electroscope is a simple device comprised of a metal rod with two thin leaves attached to one end. If the electroscope is given a negative charge, the metal leaves will separate from each other. It is the characteristic that makes the electroscope useful as a detection device. A negatively charged electroscope will discharge when ions in the air remove electrons from it, and consequently, a positively charged electroscope will discharge when it takes electrons from the air around it. The rate of discharge of the electroscope is a measure of ions in the air and can be used as a basis of measurement and detection.

Eg. Pocket Dosimeter – used to measure the accumulated dose of external radiation viz., gamma, x rays and beta radiation.

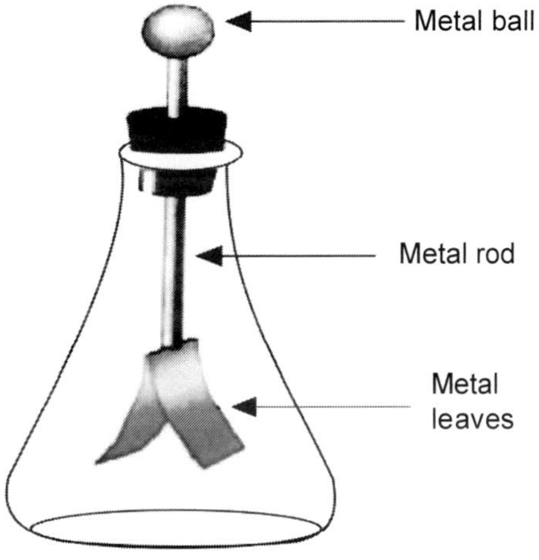

Electroscope

2. Cloud Chamber

The Cloud chamber was invented by the British physicist Charles Wilson in 1911. It is possible to see the path of ionizing radiation thus making it possible to photograph it. The cloud chamber consists of a plastic or glass container, which sits on dry ice. A dark cloth is saturated with alcohol and placed around inside of container near the top. A small radioactive material is suspended from the lid of the container. In the chamber, the alcohol evaporates from the cloth and condenses as it reaches the cold region created by the dry ice at the floor of the container. Just above the floor of the chamber there is a region where the alcohol vapor does not condense. Only seeds available in the chamber are those of ions produced by the interaction with radiation. The resulting alcohol droplets can be seen against the black background at the bottom of chamber.

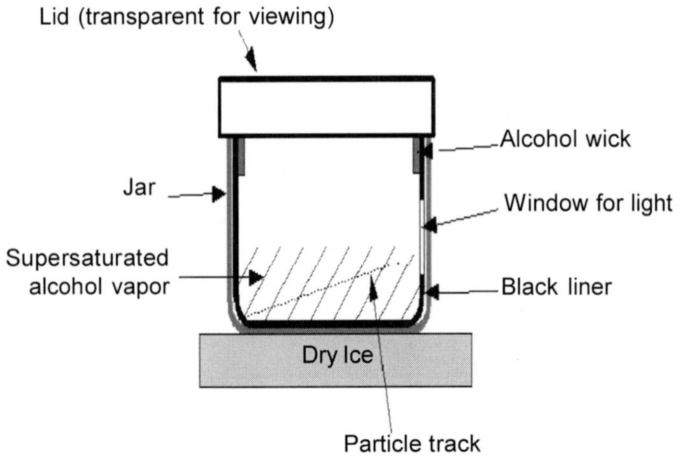

3. Ionization Chamber

Another common device used for detection and measurement is the ionization chamber. The Geiger counter, survey meter, and personal dosimeters work on the basis of the ionization chamber. The principle is that it will produce an electric current in the presence of a radioactive source. Ionization chambers consist of tubes filled with gas, such as argon. When radiation enters the tube and interacts with the gas, it removes electrons from the gas. The gas atoms become positively charged ions, and the free electrons move through the gas to a wire in the tube, setting up a current. The current is commonly amplified and sent to a recording or counting device. This in response may produce a flash of light, ticking sounds, or an analog readout. Ionization chambers are capable of measuring the amount of radiation by means of measuring the amount of current produced.

Ionizing radiation, such as X-rays, alpha rays, beta rays, and gamma rays remains undetectable by the senses, and the damage it causes to the body is cumulative, related to the total dose received.

Visualisation of ion chamber operation

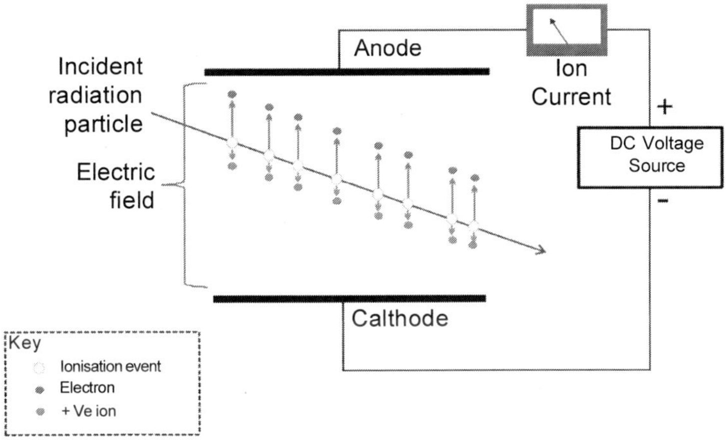

Merit

- Used for health control
- Requires low voltage for operation and can also be operated by batteries
- Have a wide range of operation
- Less sensitive to dust

Demerit

- Cannot be used for single particle detection and counting.

4. Autoradiograph

Autoradiography is a photochemical process of measuring distribution of radioactivity present in the sample. It is a self portrait and a method of visualization of the uptake and translocation of nutrients in crop plants. An autoradiograph is an image on an X-ray film or nuclear emulsion produced by the pattern of decay emissions (e.g., beta particles or gamma rays) from a distribution of a radio active substance. Autoradiograph makes use of the radiation capable of darkening the photographic plates and photographic emulsions. Radiation interacts with Si halides and the amount of metallic halide present is proportional to radiation. It is a qualitative method but also converted to semi quantitative by densitometers.

5. Photographic film

Photographic film is one of the first radiation detectors widely used for radiation sensing. Small crystals of silver halide (usually silver bromide) are suspended in a gelatin base. Ionizing radiations passing through the film produce free electrons which are trapped in the crystal lattice structure of the film and reduce the silver ions. When the film is developed, silver bromide that contains silver ions is converted to grains of metallic silver. If there is sufficient number of grains developed, the film will appear to be blackened. The degree of blackening can be quantified with appropriate calibration to give an estimate of the radiation exposure.

6. Luminescent dosimeters

These are based on the principle that certain substances which are not normally luminescent when treated by prior exposure to ionizing radiation, exhibit luminescence. In a typical photo luminescence system, silver containing meta phosphate glass is exposed to radiation. When the silver atoms are exposed to light, they absorb energy and fluorescence upon returning to stable ground state. The fluorescence may be measured and the radiation is detected.

B. Radiation Measurement Devices

Beta and gamma rays are commonly used in biological research. Beta rays are detected by Geiger Muller counter, proportional counters, liquid scintillation counter and gamma rays by solid scintillation counters.

1. Geiger Muller Counter (Beta rays with high energy)

Principle

Ionizing radiation from radioactive sample interacts with the helium gas in GM tube and produces ion pairs (electrons and positively charged ions of He atoms). When an electric potential is supplied externally, the ion pairs move towards the respective electrodes, electrons move to anode and positively charged He ions move to cathode. The movement of ion pairs create an electric pulse and eventually an electric current and is measured by a scaler. Each electric pulse marks the entry of one beta particle into the tube and is recorded in an automatic counter. The number of such pulses registered by a radioactive material per minute gives the intensity of its radioactivity.

Components of GM counter

Geiger Muller counter consists of 4 different parts viz. GM tube, Scaler, timer and sample keeping shelves.

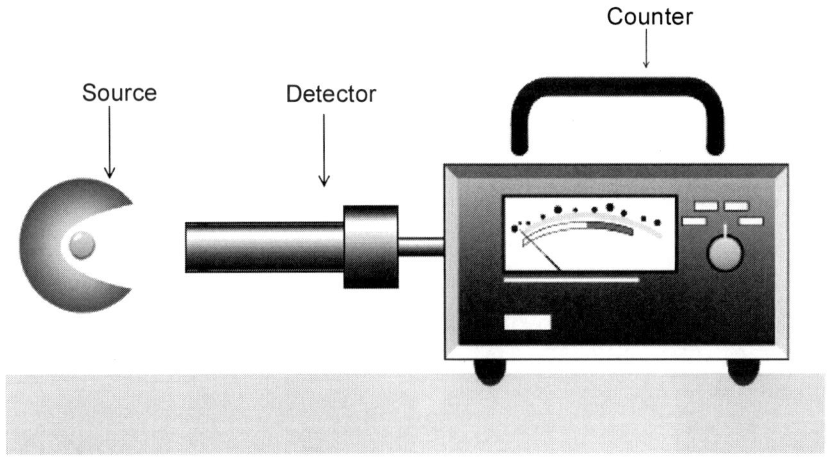

a. GM tube

It is a cylindrical tube made of glass or metal, which is coated internally with conducting material such as silver or graphite. This acts as a cathode. A thin wire, usually made of tungsten is sealed concentrically at one end of the tube and acts as anode. The GM tube is filled with noble gases such as helium or neon or argon at a pressure (0.1 atm) slightly lesser than atmospheric pressure.

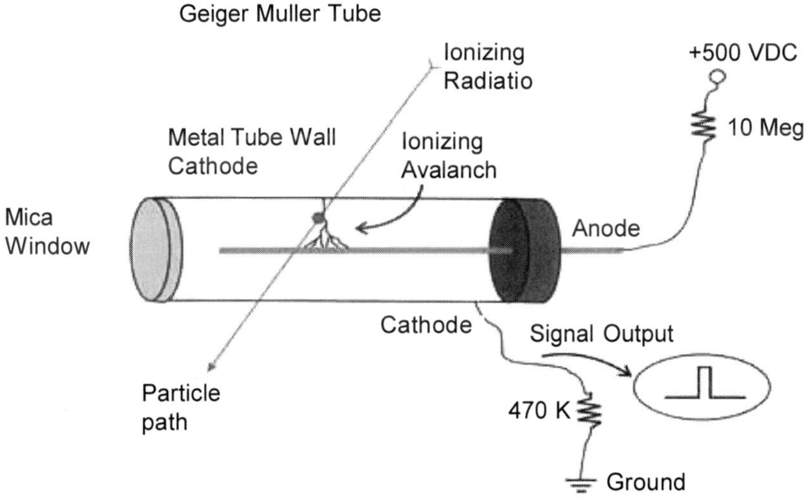

b. Scaler

Supplies high voltage necessary for the movement of ion pairs to the irrespective electrodes and supplies current to the electronic addition machine which counts radiation (each pulse) as it is detected. If high voltage is not supplied externally, the ion pairs will re combine and form neutral atoms.

c. Timer: Records the time spent in counting

d. Sample keeping shelves

If the radioactivity is too high it is advisable to keep the sample in lower windows to avoid intense ionization process which will interfere with counting. If the sample activity is predicted low it can be placed in upper windows to effect the ionization process. Usually the second shelf is taken as the reference shelf.

2.Solid scintillation counting in Gamma ray spectrometer (Gamma rays)

Principle

Gamma rays interact with matter and make the atoms to go into excited state and when the atoms are de-excited, the excess energy is released as a flash of light called scintillation. The scintillations produced are collected at photocathode where electrons are emitted by photo electric effect. These electrons are multiplied or amplified by series of dynodes in photomultiplier tube, which finally results in an electric pulse and is recorded by scaler.

Components

Gamma ray spectrophotometer consists of a scintillator, photo multipliertube, scaler and timer.

Working module

When certain materials (scintillators) are exposed to gamma photons or particulate radiation they emit scintillation or flashes of light and are called scintillators. Scintillations are produced by a complex process involving the production of an excited (higher energy) state of atoms of the material. Sodium iodide with trace of thalium iodide is used as a scintillator. The scintillations produced from the interaction of gamma rays with scintillator are collected at the photocathode of photomultiplier tube. A photo multiplier tube is an evacuated glass tube containing a series of dynodes, which are positive electrodes of increasing potential.

The photoelectrons released from the photocathode will be attracted to the first dynode stage and will gain sufficient kinetic energy to release two or more secondary electrons from the first dynode. The net result is the gain or amplification of electrons which is recorded by scaler.

3. Liquid scintillation counting (Beta rays with low energy)

Liquid scintillation counting holds good for low energy beta emitters like ^{3}H and ^{14}C. The intimate contact of liquid scintillator and sample, in which every radioactive molecule is surrounded by molecules of scintillator enhances the efficiency of counting. Quenching is the process which leads to decrease in the amount of light reaching the photocathode of the photomultiplier tube. The light absorbing properties of some biological materials in the sample reduce the amount of light reaching the photomultiplier thus reducing the counting efficiency. Chemical quenching also occur when reaction between the sample and the scintillation mixture takes place. This quenching effect is overcome in practice by the use of internal standards.

4. Semi Conductor Detector (Gamma rays)

A semiconductor detector is a device that uses a semiconductor (usually silicon or germanium) to detect traversing of charged particles or the absorption of photons. These detectors are usually known as silicon detectors. A semi conductor is a substance whose electrical conductivity is between that of a metal and an insulator. It is found that Ge (Li) semi conductors are excellent detectors of gamma rays with a resolution ten times higher than NaI(Th) scintillometers.

Radiological Safety

Radiation protection can be divided into

i. **Occupational radiation protection**- is the protection of workers

ii. **Medical radiation protection**- is the protection of patients and the radiographer and

iii. **Public radiation protection**- which is the protection of individual members of the public, and of the population as a whole.

Radiation exposure can be managed by a combination of these factors:

1. **Time:** Reducing the time of exposure reduces the effective dose proportionally.
2. **Distance:** Increasing distance reduces dose due to the inverse square law. It is the handling a source with forceps rather than fingers.
3. **Shielding:** The term 'biological shield' refers to a mass of absorbing material placed around a reactor, or other radioactive source, to reduce the radiation to a level safe for humans. In x-ray facilities, the plaster on the rooms with the x-ray generator contains barium sulfate and the operators stay behind a leaded glass screen and wear lead aprons.
4. **Amount** - Reduce the quantity of radioactive material for a practice.

Safety measures in radio isotope laboratories

- Site location and arrangement of lab to be in the ground floor, no radioactive waste material should be released into the environment.
- Area inside the lab should be segregated depending upon the operation and activity. Low activity should be carried out at one end and high activity at the other end. The counting facility should be housed in a separate room.
- Flooring should not be porous. It should be covered with rubber tiles, vinyl tiles, linoleum, asphalt etc.
- Walls should be coated with washable non porous painting.
- Sharp corners must be rounded off for easy cleaning.
- Work surfaces should be covered with polythene sheets (or absorbent papers) subsequently these papers should be destroyed.
- There should be enough ventilation. The flow of air should be from low to high activity.
- Furniture should be easily washable. Sinks should be glazed.
- The lab should have a hot cell to receive, work and store the radioactive material.
- Cross contamination between labs should be avoided and the lab be air conditioned.

Handling procedures

- Use thin rubber gloves
- Avoid pipetting with mouth. Use remote pipetting device
- Open wound below the wrist – not to be allowed.
- Labels requiring wetting to be avoided
- Special foot operated waste bins to be used.

Special equipments

- Use radio chemical fume hood when gaseous reactions are involved.
- Use of glove box. It is a dust tight box fitted with window in which manipulation with hazardous α, β materials can be done. It is an enclosed equipment which isolates air inside from that the outside. This is suitable for handling toxic substances especially suited for dry and dusty operation.

Contamination monitoring devices

- Hand and clothing monitors, contamination monitors, field survey meters- all battery operated should be used to monitor the contamination.

Radiation protection appliances

- Lead bricks, lead aprons, lead loaded gloves, goggles, face mask, nose cover, gum boots, remote handling pipette, remote handling tongs should be used.

Rules and Regulations

- Unauthorised entry to be prevented.
- Everyone should wear lab coat and personal monitoring badge
- When work is completed each person should individually clean or dispose off the contaminated material.
- Use always rubber gloves and wash the hands thoroughly and monitor with the help of suitable instruments before leaving the lab.
- Should not eat, smoke or chew in the lab.

- Visitors also should wear aprons.
- Personal monitoring badges should be worn

Lab Working

- Lab should be periodically monitored and cleaned. All radioactive wastes should be collected in a foot operated container marked with radiation symbol.
- All persons working in a lab should be well informed about radiation control measures.

Radiation hazards

- The harmful effects are due to their ionizing properties. The radiations first generate either atoms, or free radicals or excited molecules by interaction with matter. These materials are chemically very active and undergo number of secondary processes with various molecules in the living cells, resulting in the inhibition of certain essential enzymes and their behaviour.
- The changes produced by radiation can be somatic - experienced by the exposed individual or genetic - observed not by the exposed individual but by his later generations. The somatic effects may be felt immediately within a short time interval (or) few years.
- If the radiation is received in one large dose it is acute. If received in repeated doses over a prolonged time leading to cumulative effect, it is called chronic dose.

Symptoms

- Early symptoms are vomiting, prostration, loss of appetite, loss of weight, fewer rapid heart action, severe diarrhoea, bleeding gums, loss of hair etc. In severe cases, white blood cells are affected resulting in life shortening, leukemia, cancer, cataracts etc.
- Radioisotopes like Ca, Sr and Ba accumulate in the bones as they are bone seekers.
- Materials like iodine 131 accumulates in thyroid leading to necrosis and tumor formation.

Radiation exposure units

- **Roentgen (R) -** It is the quantity of X-ray or gamma ray that produces one electrostatic unit of charge in one cubic centimeter of air. The roentgen is therefore a measure of the ionizing effect of the radiation.

- **Radiation absorbed dose (rad) -** One rad can be considered equal to one R. It is defined as 100 ergs/g of any type of radiation.
- **Roentgen equivalent mass (rem) -** The product of Radiation Absorbed Dose (RAD) with the quality factor (Q) of the radiation is called as rem.
- **Milli rem (mrem) -** One in thousandth of a rem is one mrem.
- **Milli Gray (mGy) -** A newer international unit, the Gray to replace rad 1 rad = ImGy
- **Milli Sievert (mSv) -** Another newer international unit, to replace the rem. 1 rem = 10 mSv.

Shielding techniques for different radiations

- Alpha particles (helium nuclei) are the least penetrating which can be stopped by a single sheet of paper.
- Beta particles (electrons) are more penetrating, but can be absorbed by a few millimeters of aluminum, plastic, wood, water or acrylic glass.
- X-rays and gamma radiations are shielded by lead and barium sulphate
- Ultraviolet (UV) radiation is ionizing but it is not penetrating, so it can be shielded by thin opaque layers such as sunscreen, clothing, and protective eyewear.

International agencies associated with Radiation

- ICRP - International Commission on Radiation Protection
- IAEA- International Atomic Energy Agency
- NCRP- National Council on Radiation Protection and Measurements, USA
- IRPA - International Radiation Protection Association

Exposure limits

The US nuclear regulatory commission and agreement states have given the occupational guidelines for lifetime.

Permissible lifetime dose = 5 (N -18) (rems)

where N is age of individual, Yearly occupational exposure limit is 5 rem /year. For pregnant women, it is 500 m rem / entire pregnancy.

Chapter 17

Applications of Stable and Radioactive Isotopes in Agricultural Research

Stable isotopes are chemical isotopes that may or may not be radioactive,but if radioactive, have half-lives too long to be measured. These isotopes decay into stable products. Eg. ^{14}C having 6protons and electrons with 8 neutrons.

Most elements of biological interest (including C, H, O, N, and S) have two or more stable isotopes. Among the stable isotopes, the most useful as biological tracers are the heavy isotopes of carbon and nitrogen.

Average terrestrial abundances of the stable isotopes

Element isotope abundance (%)

Hydrogen ^{1}H 99.985

^{2}H 0.015

Carbon ^{12}C 98.89

^{13}C 1.11

Nitrogen ^{14}N 99.63

^{15}N 0.37

Oxygen ^{16}O 99.759

^{17}O 0.037

^{18}O 0.204

Sulfur ^{32}S 95.00

^{33}S 0.76

^{34}S 4.22

^{36}S 0.014

Atom Percent

Atoms ^{15}N

Atom% ^{15}N = x 100

Atoms ^{14}N + Atoms ^{15}N

Atoms ^{13}C

Atom% ^{13}C = x 100

Atoms ^{12}C + Atoms ^{13}C

Applications

Following are the fields where stable isotopes are used to understand the nutrient behaviour in soil.

a. Tracing studies

Nitrogen cycling: To investigate nitrogen cycling in crop plants, ^{15}N-labelled fertilizer (urea, ammonium nitrate) either 2-5% enriched or 0.36% depleted in ^{15}N is applied. Following the tracer studies, the fate of added fertilizer N viz., portion taken up by the plants, remaining in the soil N pool, lost by denitrification into the atmosphere, and leached into runoff waters etc. can be quantified. Such data helps to make fertilizer recommendations to increase the yield and reduce the groundwater pollution.

b. Fractionation studies

Nitrogen fixation: Soil N is often more abundant in ^{15}N than in atmosphere. The non-N-fixing plants obtain their nitrogen from soil while N-fixing plants fix atmospheric nitrogen which will differ in their ^{15}N values. This difference forms the basis for estimating symbiotic N by ^{15}N natural abundance technique.

Photosynthesis and carbon cycling: Terrestrial plants fix atmospheric $CO_2$by two main photosynthetic reaction pathways viz., C_3- the Calvin-Benson, and C_4 - the Hatch-Slack. C_3plants convert atmospheric CO_2 to a phospho glycerate compound with three C atoms while C_4 plants convert $CO_2$to dicarboxylic acid, a four-C compound. ^{13}C value is a standard method for distinguishing C_3 and C_4plant groups and is used by plant physiologists to determine drought resistance in C_3 plants, as well as to breed for improvement in this increasingly vital characteristic.

c. Archaeological investigations

The characteristic isotope-ratio "signatures" of food species are passed on to consumers. It is possible to determine the proportion of C_3 and

C_4 plant species in the diet of herbivores and to make inferences about the prey species selected by carnivores.

d. Ecological and Environmental research

Many stable isotopes are used in these fields and are referred as natural abundance isotope technique.

Eg. Intake of CO_2 containing lighter carbon isotope ($^{12}C\text{-}CO_2$) in photosynthesis

Other stable isotope techniques which rely on adding trace amount of compounds that are artificially enriched in rare isotope of the element of interest are known as isotope tracer techniques.

Eg. $^{15}NH_4$ in N mineralization studies

- Base of food web - ^{13}C, ^{34}S
- Causes of Nitrate and Sulphate pollution - ^{15}N, ^{34}S, ^{18}O
- Water use efficiency of plants – ^{13}C
- Source of water to plants – ^{18}O,^{2}H
- Quantity of N added through fixation – ^{15}N
- Rates of carbon and N turnover in soil – ^{13}C, ^{15}N
- CO_2 production by plants roots and soil microorganisms – ^{13}C, ^{18}O
- N_2O production by Nitrifiers and denitrifiers – ^{15}N , ^{18}O

e. Correction of Carbon-14 dates

Since carbon is strongly fractionated by biological processes, it is not possible to date ancient carbon-bearing material by the carbon-14method. If biological samples selectively accumulate heavy C isotopes, this will make them appear young. Stable isotope analysis gives an independent measure of fractionation.

Mass spectrometry

It is the most common method of analyzing stable isotopes. **Mass spectrometry** (MS) is an analytical technique which measures the mass-to-charge ratio of charged particles. It is used for determining masses of particles, for determining the elemental composition of a sample or molecule, and for elucidating the chemical structures of molecules. This method was first used by J.J.Thompson to demonstrate the isotopic nature of neon.

Principle

The element being studied is converted to gas molecules and the atoms of the vapour are ionized by bombardment with electrons emitted from a hot filament. Ionizing of chemical compounds generate charged molecules or molecular fragments and measuring their mass-to-charge ratios

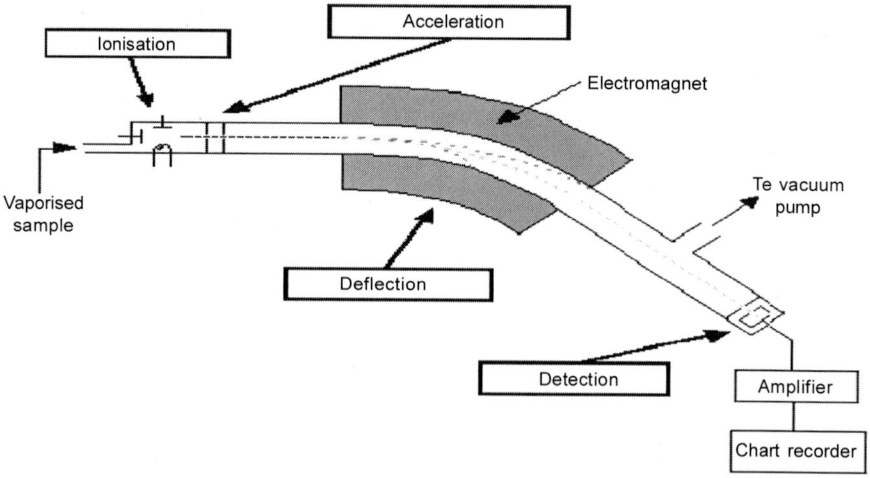

Components

- **Ion source-** which can convert gas phase sample molecules into positive ions by loss of electrons. Ions produced in the ionisation chamber move freely for creating vacuum.
- **Ionisation chamber**-The electrically heated metal coil gives off electrons which are attracted to the electron trap which is a positively charged plate. The particles in the sample are bombarded with a stream of electrons, and some of the collisions knock one or more electrons out of the sample particles to make positive ions.
- **Mass analyzer** - sorts the ions by their masses by applying electromagnetic fields following Lorentz force law and Newton's second law. It comprises of acceleration and deflection
- **Acceleration -** The positive ions are repelled away from the positive ionisation chamber and pass through three slits and the final one of which is at 0 volts. All the ions are accelerated into a finely focused beam.
- **Deflection**-Ions are deflected by the magnetic field by different amounts. The amount of deflection depends on Mass of ion - Lighter

ions are deflected more than heavier ones.Charge on ion - Ions with 2 or more positive charges are deflected more than ones with only 1 positive charge.

These two factors are combined into **mass/charge ratio.** Mass/charge ratio is given the symbol m/z.

Detector, which measures the value of an indicator quantity and thus provides data for calculating the abundances of each ion present. When an ion hits the metal box, its charge is neutralised by an electron jumping from the metal on to the ion. A flow of electrons in the wire is detected as an electric current which can be amplified and recorded. The more ions arriving, the greater the current. The machine can be calibrated to record current (which is a measure of the number of ions) against m/z directly. The mass is measured on the ^{12}C scale.

Applications

- To determine the isotopic composition of elements within a sample.
- Used in the analysis of trace gas
- Protein characterization
- Glycology, Space exploration, Respiratory gas analysis

Applications of radioactive isotopes in agriculture

Radioactive isotopes are widely used in agriculture in the field of fertilizer studies, plant nutrition, irrigation management, plant protection, post harvest studies, plant breeding etc. Alpha emitters (Ru, Pu, Po,U) are not generally used in biological studies because

- The penetration power is very less and hence it won't enter plant or human tissues
- Most of the alpha emitters are lanthanides (Uranium, Radium, Plutonium) which are not relevant to plant nutrition.

1. Nutrient movement studies

The basic advantage of isotopic technique is that the fertilizer actually taken by the crop can be detected and measured. It is possible to get precise information on the following parameters

- Optimum condition of placement of fertilizers
- Relative efficacy of major sources of different nutrients
- Amount of nutrients taken from fertilizer and soil

The methods employing radioisotopes to measure the above concepts are A value, E value and L value.

A value (Fried and Dean, 1952)

To know the amount of nutrient derived from fertilizer, the fertilizer will be tagged with a known quantity of radioisotope. For example, to study the availability of phosphorus, the fertilizer should be tagged with ^{32}P and applied to soil. The plant will take P from both soil and fertilizer. The proportion of nutrient derived form fertilizer can be found out by measuring the radioactive P present in the sample. Known quantity of plant sample should be ashed in muffle furnace and the activity of ^{32}Pin sample can be detected in GM counter / liquid scintillation counter.

A value

$$A = \frac{B\,(1 - Y)}{Y}$$

Where

A = Amount of available nutrient in soil.

B = Amount of applied fertilizer nutrient

Y = Proportion of nutrient in the plant derived from the fertilizer nutrient

E value (Russel *et al.*, 1954)

It measures the amount of nutrient in the soil that is in equilibrium with the same nutrient in soil solution.

Specific activity of added P solution

E value = % P derived from fertilizer (ìg/g soil) x Amount of P added to soil

L value (Larsen, 1952)

Amount of phosphorus in the soil solution that is exchangeable with the orthophosphate ions added to the soil as measured by plants growing in the system.

L=(Co / C -1) x Where, Co and C are specific activities of the added P and x is the amount of P added.

2. Root activity studies

It consists of injecting a solution containing a suitable isotope at various distances and depth from the base of plant in to the soil and taking the amount of isotope found in the above ground parts.

3. Root distribution studies

The plant is sprayed or injected with a solution containing a radio active isotope which is easily translocated into roots. By sampling the soil in a regular pattern as regard to distance and depth, the activity of the roots in the soil sample can be measured. Suitable isotopes are ^{32}P and ^{86}Rb (as both the elements are translocated easily)

4. Mutation breeding

It is a genetic improvement technique of crop plants for various economic characters through induced mutation. Irradiation of crops with rays from ^{60}Co can lead to change in the genetic traits of the plants due to its deep penetrating rays. Commonly used in self-pollinated and asexually propagated species and rarely used in cross pollinated crops. Mutation breeding is a cheap and rapid method of developing new varieties as compared to back cross, pedigree method and bulk breeding methods. Worldwide more than 1500 mutant cultivars of crop and ornamental plants have been released in the past 30 years.

5. Sterile male technique

There are some insects which mate only once in life. The males of such insects can be reared in the laboratory on a mass scale and sterilized by a dose of gamma rays. When such sterilized males are released in the pest infested area, they mate with their females and die. Because of sterility no new generation is born and after sometime even the females also die resulting in ultimate wiping out of the pests. Eg. Eradication of screw worm attacking the cattle in the United States.

6. Soil moisture measurement / bulk density measurement

The study of soil moisture employs ^{137}Cs gamma irradiation method. The change in bulk density occurs due to shrinkage or swelling caused by the soil moisture status which will affect gamma ray absorption. Soil erosion can be measured using ^{137}Cs as a tracer.

7. Food irradiation

Food irradiation is the process of exposing food to ionizing radiation in order to destroy bacteria, viruses or insects which are present in the food. It is also used for sprout inhibition, delay in ripening, increase juice content and improvement of rehydration. Gamma rays, X rays and electrons are involved in food irradiation processes. Low dose (upto to 1 KGy), medium dose (1KGy to 10 KGy) and high doses(above 10 KGy) are used in food irradiation.

8. Plant protection

Radio isotopes are used for conducting ecological studies, metabolic reactions in animals and plants, pesticide residues in plant and soil. Movement of vectors has been identified with the help of labeled compounds. Translocation of herbicides and their metabolism in sterilizing the insects have been studied with the help of radioisotopes.

9. Radiocarbon (C^{14}) Dating

Radio carbon dating technique is frequently useful in archaeology, anthropology, oceanography, pedology, climatology and geology.

$C^{14}$is a radioactive isotope of carbon, with a half life of **5860** years. It is continuously created through collisions of neutrons generated by cosmic rays with nitrogen in the upper atmosphere.

$$^{14}N_7 + {^1}n_o \text{ ------------- } {^{14}}C_6 + {^1}H_1$$

Being radioactive, carbon-14 disintegrate into nitrogen by the emission of beta particles (electrons).

$$^{14}C_6 \text{ ------------- } {^{14}}N_7 + {^0}e_{-1}$$

The percentage of ^{14}C and ^{12}C is more or less constant in atmosphere. All living organisms continue to absorb C during their life cycle and have therefore radiocarbon ^{14}C& normal ^{12}C atom combinations in their systems. When the organism dies there is no further absorption of C (as either ^{12}C or ^{14}C), but carbon atoms of both types undergo chemical reactions. In the process of decomposition, the ^{14}C atoms continue to disintegrate into nitrogen by beta emission. ^{12}C does not undergo any nuclear change. Thus the ratio of ^{14}C atoms steadily decreases. From the ratio of ^{14}C and ^{12}C, it is possible to calculate the age of the organism.

10. Ozone depletion studies

Beryllium-7(^{7}Be) and Beryllium-10 (^{10}Be) are used in ozone depletion studies. These beryllium isotopes are created in the stratosphere when cosmic rays strike nitrogen atoms. Aerosol particles in the atmosphere serve as host sites for chemical reactions which create the forms of chlorine that destroy ozone. Since beryllium isotopes attach readily to aerosols, they are helping scientists to understand aerosol movement in the atmosphere.

Chapter 18

Use of Radioactive and Stable Isotopes in Analytical Applications

The two principal nuclear methods are of interest in analytical applications are:

1. Activation analysis
2. Radioactive tracer methods.
    - Isotopic dilution methods
    - Radiometric analysis methods.

1. Neutron activation analysis

This technique is used in qualitative and quantitative analysis. If an element present in a sample is to be identified by neutron activation analysis, the sample will be bombarded with slow neutrons or other charged particles and converted into radioisotope. It is one of the most sensitive and specific methods available for the determination of trace quantities of a wide range of elements. From the half life measurement, it is possible to identify the element from which the radioisotope has resulted. Also the quantity of element present in a given sample can be calculated by this technique.

The steps involved in the complete analysis by neutron activation are:

- Activation of the sample
- Identification and/or isolation of the nuclide, identification very often requires a chemical separation.
- Quantitative assay for the nuclide

Advantages

- Non-destructive technique which does not require any removal from the sample to be analysed.

- Highly sensitive and permits quantitative determination of elements present in traces.
- It is a simple alternative to much more tedious procedures.

Limitations

1. Not suitable for elements having very short half life.

   Eg. He, Li, B, W, O and Ne (Half life is few seconds) and Al, Mg, Ti, V and Nb (Half life is few minutes).

2. **Physical limitations:** Heat is also produced during neutron bombardment in a nuclear reactor, hence samples must withstand high temperature.

3. **Chemical limitations:** Samples put into a nuclear reactor will be bombarded both by gamma-rays and neutrons. Structural damage and decomposition occurs.

   Eg.Silica becomes almost black after a few hours of irradiation.

4. **Nuclear limitations:** Sample must not have high neutron absorption during irradiation.

5. **Radioactive nuclide** which is used as a measure of mass of a given element may be formed from different elements present in the sample is to be estimated.

Eg. Determination of arsenic by reactor irradiation depends on the formation of As^{76} from the mono isotopic $As^{75}$by the nuclear reaction.

$$_{33}As^{75} + {}_{0}n^{1} \rightarrow {}_{33}As^{76}$$

However,As^{76} can be formed by several other reactions starting which elements present in the sample to be analysed other than arsenic:

$$_{34}Se^{76} + {}_{0}n^{1} \rightarrow {}_{33}As^{76} + {}_{1}H^{1}$$

$$_{35}Br^{77} + {}_{0}n^{1} \rightarrow {}_{33}As^{76} + 2\ {}_{1}H^{1}$$

Applications

- Sensitive method for detecting impurities in construction material and moderators in nuclear reactors.
- Trace elements like Zn, Cu, Mn and Co present in rocks, soils and meteorites can be estimated.
- Used in dating geological specimens.

- Recently utilized for the analysis of compositions in lunar surface by Americans
- Highly useful in the nondestructive analysis of rare archaeological artifacts
- Utilized to identify the geographic origin of specimen of pottery.
- Used in human studies- This revealed that human hair contains several trace elements which are characteristics to the individual from whom the hair has been taken.

2. Isotope dilution analysis

It is an example of radiometric method of trace analysis. It is used to determine the quantity of constituent (radioactive or non-radioactive) in a mixture of closely related compounds which are difficult to separate and to estimate quantitatively using conventional methods. The radioactivity of the known weight of radioactive compound is measured. To the unknown mixture, a known weight of the radioactive compound is added. The radioactive and nonradioactive varieties of the compound have identical chemical properties. The compound is then separated from the mixture. The separated product contains both radioactive and non radioactive compounds. The activity of the known weight of the radioactive compound shows the inactive compound present in the mixture.

Types of isotopic dilution methods

There are four types of Isotopic dilution methods and are based on same fundamental principle but differ in technique and procedure and are applied under different circumstances

(a) Direct isotopic dilution method

This method is used to determine the quantity of non- radio active substance in a mixture of closely related substance which is difficult to separate quantitatively by usual conventional methods.

(b) Inverse isotopic dilution method

As the name implies, inverse isotopic dilution is essentially the reverse of direct isotopic dilution. It is only applicable when a system contains an unknown amount of an isotopically labeled substance, i.e., a radioactive substance of specific activity (S).

(c) Double isotope dilution method

This technique has been used particularly in biochemistry where simple quantitative chemical separation methods are frequently not available. This does not require a knowledge of specific activity 'S' of the unknown substance.

(d) Modified inverse isotopic dilution method

This procedure is same as that of inverse isotopic dilution method, except radioactive substance which is determined by a second radioactive substance. This method is used when a stable isotope is un available or its use is undesirable, procedures involving polonium and palladium are typical examples.

Applications

1. Zinc, copper, mercury, indium and other cations can be determined by this method as low as 10^{-9} to 10^{-10} g.
2. Used to determine the volume of water in the body by using radioactive tritium as a tracer.
3. Useful in analyzing the mixture of amino acids resulting from the chemical hydrolysis of protein outside the body by using labeled amino acids containing N^{15} to act as the tracer.

3. Radiometric analysis

Radioactive iodine is used to prepare radioactive Potassium iodide (KI). It is used to calculate the quantity of silver (Ag) present in the sample. Different concentrations of silver nitrate solutions are prepared and silver is precipitated as AgI by adding an excess of KI solution. Radioactivity of AgI is measured and a graph is plotted between the quantity of AgI and its radioactivity. This is called calibration graph.

A known volume of the given silver nitrate solution is taken and radioactive KI is added. Thus AgI is formed and its radioactivity is measured. The quantity of AgI is computed with the help of calibration graph. From the weight of AgI, the quantity of Ag present in the sample solution can be calculated.

4. Radiometric titration

The end-point of the reaction is obtained by plotting the changes in the radioactivity against the amount of titrant added. Because a linear relation exists between concentration of the labeled substance and radioactivity, the titration curve is also linear. The end-point is obtained by the point of intersection of the two linear proportions of the titration curve. In the titration of chloride solution with labeled $AgNO_3$solution taken in the burette, when a small volume of $AgNO_3$is added, is converted into AgCl which carries the radioactive silver. The radioactivity is in AgCl which settles down and the supernatant liquid does not have any radioactivity. After the equivalence point, the addition of radioactive $AgNO_3$solution will be detected in the supernatant liquid. Thus the point at which the supernatant liquid shows radioactivity is the end point of titration.

Applications

- Determining the composition of compounds formed during titration
- Used to investigate co precipitation
- Determine the specific activity of radioactive preparations

Advantages

- End-point can be established much more accurately than conventional coloured organic indicators.
- Readily used in automatic analysis
- Titrations can be carried out in heterogeneous, coloured, turbid, corrosive or non-aqueous system because radioactivity is not affected by these conditions.